Praise

'Hybrid Selling takes a fre
selling in the new millennium. ine EVOLVE Model,
which is explained in detail, provides an excellent
framework for improving sales effectiveness and
efficiency. New sales representatives and seasoned
sales professionals will find value in reading this
book and applying its modern principles.'
> — **Tom Williams**, founder of *Strategic Dynamics*
> and author of *Buyer Centred Selling*
> and *The Seller's Challenge*

'I absolutely love the format. The dialogue between
Harry and Larry is superb and really reflects the
day-to day-conversations we have all had at some
point.'
> — **Malvina El-Sayegh**, Head of Sales
> Enablement, Silverfin, and #StayHuman
> podcast host

'I like the use of a framework: the EVOLVE model.
It's simple and catchy. I love the use of a story with
dialogue that is also chronological throughout a sales
year. The book covers a wide range of very important
and relevant aspects of modern selling. I like this
very much and especially how the chapters flow
when considering each one of these areas.'
> — **Moeed Amin**, founder of Proverbial Door

'Chock full of B2B sales insights for the new age, *Hybrid Selling* couldn't be more relevant for our newly changed world of selling. It's oozing with salient advice along with new and modernised strategies for sales professionals. It's an easy read that is both practical and entertaining. I highly recommend it.'

    — **James Muir**, CEO and founder of
        Best Practice International and author of
        The Perfect Close

MIKE

FRED COPESTAKE

HYBRID SELLING

HOW SALESPEOPLE CAN
USE A COMPLETE APPROACH
TO DRIVE OPPORTUNITIES IN THE
NEW WORLD OF SALES

Thanks for all your support
Hope you enjoy this
(especially the Value bit)

Re think

First published in Great Britain in 2021 by Rethink Press (www.rethinkpress.com)

For Tilly

You sat on my desk while I was writing this
– stay there a little longer

Mum – I wish you could have read this

Contents

Foreword

Buckle up! You're in for a ride.

The worlds of buying and selling have changed profoundly in the past several years. Much of this change has been driven by huge shifts in customers' buying behaviours, with over 80% of customers preferring to buy with minimal sales help. This, in addition to the pandemic, has forced customers to change how they buy (and they like it!), forcing salespeople to engage with customers differently.

What worked before still works – kinda.

But we've discovered new ways of selling and engaging our customers. Before the COVID-19 pandemic happened, I had never heard of virtual selling. I thought Zoom was something airplanes and rockets did. Before the pandemic, face to face dominated our engagement strategies and we felt good when we could meet with two or three different customers a day. Today, I have a minimum of six different customer meetings each day, and most of the time it's far more.

Never have we had to adapt so profoundly and quickly in order to achieve our goals. We are having to learn what parts of what we have always done still make sense, and what new methods, tools and processes we need to adapt to deal with what we now face.

The concept of hybrid selling is coming to the forefront. It's a mix of things that have been (and continue to be) very impactful, along with new approaches we've discovered in this period of turbulence. It's all based on the same basic principles of creating value in every interaction, understanding our customers' businesses and developing trusting relationships.

My first impression when reading Fred's book was similar to that of drinking from a firehose. He presents so much in relatively few pages. When I was finished, I felt a little overwhelmed. All of it is important. All of it is critical to our success as sales professionals. But there was so much! And that's the reality we face in adapting to this new world of buying and selling.

I knew the concepts introduced in the book were important. I took the time to reread it. Everything started making so much more sense. I started to understand how all the different things Fred introduces fit together. I could now start mapping a new way forward in adopting the principles and approaches outlined in the book.

What we face can seem overwhelming. I don't know how much Fred intended this when he wrote the book, but it reflects reality and that is... overwhelming.

But do this – read it a second time. You will vividly see how everything outlined makes sense. Everything starts fitting together and you can start to map a course forward to help your customers navigate their own challenging times, and more effectively exploit the concepts of hybrid selling.

Again, buckle up. You are in for a ride. One that is important for your customers, for your company and for your ongoing success!

David Brock, CEO at Partners in Excellence, and author of *Sales Manager Survival Guide*

Introduction

'What a time to be in sales!'

I've heard people say this various times in many different ways – excited, exasperated, worried, pessimistic, optimistic, happy, sad, confused – the whole range of human emotions.

This is an exciting time to be in sales, if you are selling B2B complex solutions. It's a time when you can bring huge value to your customers; it's a time to thrive. But you need to know how, as it is a time unlike any before. The rules have changed and as a sales professional you can have a hand in redefining how the game is played.

I have been in and around sales since the age of 8, when I started 'helping out' in the family business at the Boxing Day sale. Twenty-two years ago, I founded a sales training consultancy and have travelled round the world fourteen times visiting thirty-six countries and worked with over 10,000 salespeople. I have delivered projects that range from implementing a European academy for a leading beer brand, via developing sales skills in the Middle East for global healthcare companies, to introducing account development and sales leadership models in Latin America and Europe for IT and engineering multinationals.

This experience has been invaluable in understand the things that really make a difference in modern selling, and I addressed these in my first book *Selling Through Partnering Skills – a modern approach to winning business* (AuthorHouse, 2020). These ideas form the basis of my work with sales professionals involved in complex B2B sales, to develop their approach and ensure it is up to date and has maximum impact.

Challenges salespeople face can be broadly summarised as:

- 'Busy Busy Busy' – this is being ineffective; it results in wasted opportunities, is tiring and stressful and means the focus is on the wrong activities to deliver results.

- 'Olde Worlde' – this is being old-fashioned; when salespeople are self-centred rather than customer-focused, too technical in their approach or use bad techniques better suited to a bygone era of selling.

- 'Muddled Mindset' – this is being misaligned; it can happen at organisation, management and individual level and the confusion leads to frustration and wasted effort.

By using a more collaborative approach salespeople can make a difference and sales can become a force for good and fight against the negative image it can often be associated with.

Yet the world of sales changes at pace and recent developments make it more important than ever to rapidly adapt to new ways of working. This means that for salespeople to stay relevant they need to master these things quickly.

The danger is that as this speed of change increases the challenges salespeople face will be amplified, and those who cannot respond will be outpaced by their competition and excluded by customers from opportunities and discussions to which it is perceived they can add little or no value.

Hybrid Selling – How salespeople can use a complete approach to drive opportunities in the new world of sales shows you how to adapt, master new developments and stay in front.

Many people think hybrid selling is about using technology – such as virtual conferencing, video messaging and social media, along with tools that harness the power of artificial intelligence. And it is, but it also goes way beyond that. Focusing only on these is a mistake as potentially you will miss the other evolutions that salespeople should consider to be of real value for customers.

The **EVOLVE** model drives the right thinking to do the right things. It gives a framework and content that work in today's and tomorrow's sales environments. It provides a means for salespeople to have immediate impact and to futureproof themselves. Customers under increasing pressure will give their time and attention to those that communicate with them and demonstrate an understanding of their world.

The EVOLVE model equips salespeople to do this by addressing:

1. **Essentials** for success. These include understanding and selling benefits, prospecting, managing sales calls, writing proposals and presenting live. These activities are still fundamentally the basis for good, solid selling.

2. **Virtual selling** and the associated skills are now part and parcel of the way that we operate. Virtual selling, for the purposes of this book, is about how we can operate using the tools and

the techniques that are given to us by modern technology.

3. **Opportunity management** is different to account management but there are plenty of similarities. It focuses on a specific project or an identified chance to win business. It is all about information. It is understanding what we know and what we don't know. If we recognise that we have things we need to understand better, we can take steps to find out and make better decisions.

4. **Leading** – Salespeople are change agents and should think and act as such. They should challenge the status quo. We want customers to do things differently and we know it is not always easy for them. The more comfortable we are with change ourselves, the easier it will be for us to help customers manage their changes. We can start to talk about change as an opportunity.

5. **Value selling** – This is not particularly new: there has been a focus on value selling for at least twenty years. However, that does not make it any less important today. As salespeople, we must understand what value is. But, as a colleague of mine often says, 'It's a mystery.' We don't really know what value is until we work out what it means *to the customer*. Once this is established, we can share insights and ways of working that are going to help them.

6. **Expanding** relationships and reach. This is what
   we do as professional salespeople. A concept
   often talked about is 'land and expand'. Though
   it may sound a bit manipulative, it is not, and it
   makes sense. Expanding a relationship is about
   starting off on a project, working on some initial
   opportunities and delivering on those by ensuring
   the customer enjoys the success they are seeking.
   So naturally, the whole relationship starts to
   develop, and this is not a bad thing. It is what
   both parties want.

This book will provide you with a solid understanding so you can operate in the new selling environment
and give a solid approach to winning real business
opportunities.

We begin with a story about two fictional salespeople,
Harry and Larry. It is fiction, but it is based in reality.
Maybe you will recognise yourself.

In Part 2 I break down the EVOLVE model and provide content designed to drive action – real-life sales
activity.

The final Part is all about you. A self-assessment is
provided, which is designed to help you to gauge
where you are now so you can focus and measure
your progress in implementing hybrid selling.

The opportunities for success are huge for those who can make the necessary adjustments. As will become clear, this may be building on and refining capabilities you already have, though it may require developing new skills. What is certain is that it is worth the effort, and the time is now – *carpe diem*!

What a time to be in sales…

PART ONE
WHEN HARRY MET LARRY

'Are you sitting comfortably? Then we'll begin.'

This was the phrase used to introduce stories on the BBC radio programme *Listen With Mother* between 1950 and 1982.

I'm going to start this book with a play for two sales-people, as an opportunity for readers to reflect on their own experience.

This is about how they cope with challenges that come their way through a unique set of circumstances. It is intended to introduce ideas and some of the central concepts of hybrid selling, which are then explored in more detail in Part 2 of the book.

Once upon a time…

1

The Future Looks Bright

December 2019

This story is all about when Harry met Larry. Basically, it's a short play about hybrid selling, but before we go into that, let's go back to the very beginning. The story started in 2019, at the end of the year. Harry and Larry had a habit of getting together and reflecting on the previous twelve months.

But before we start, Harry and Larry are two guys who have been in sales a little while. They're both pretty successful and they like to meet up and chat about what they have been up to, share ideas and generally support each other.

Here's how the conversation went when they met just before Christmas 2019.

HARRY: You know what, Larry, I think we've had a pretty good ten years at this sales malarkey.

LARRY: Yeah, we have. It's been pretty cool. We've learned, and we've earned. Let's think about all the stuff we've done.

HARRY: Yeah, let's. Can you remember that very first training session that we went on, where we met? Where was it? Somewhere in the middle of the UK, I think. It's where we learned all the basics of sales.

LARRY: Oh yeah. That was really cool. I remember that training course. Can you remember how that first night went?

HARRY: Yes, I can. Oh dear, I don't need reminding of it. Let's think about the stuff that we covered.

LARRY: Ah, OK. Yeah, it was a good night, you're right. But really the stuff that we learned back then, the essentials for success, it was amazing. It's set us up for the last ten years, hasn't it? Now, what did we cover? We started with benefit selling: the difference between features, advantages, benefits... and that customers only really buy what's in it for them, that they have to appreciate how they can get something from what it is we're selling. Otherwise, what's the point? And it's our job to be able to articulate this and to be able to help people understand it well. That is the basis for sales, isn't it really?

HARRY: Absolutely. There's no point really in going out and prospecting if we don't understand that, and if we can't help customers, what would be the point? Prospecting though, that's changed, hasn't it? It used to be pure cold calling, but now there are so many different things involved.

LARRY: You're right. But the basis is still the same. I mean, really, we've got to be thinking what we can do for customers and how can we get that message across so we can set up a decent meeting.

HARRY: Decent meetings, yeah, absolutely. The various elements to them. I mean, who knew there were so many parts to them? You know, building rapport and recognising people's personality styles, how we open up to get people's attention, how we then show interest in people by asking them questions to really understand them, to uncover their needs and their wants, how we then put together our ideas in a way that's relevant to them… And then, to make sure we close, to make sure we get some kind of advancement in the sale to keep things moving. There's a lot to it and I think many people don't really understand that that's what professional sales is about.

LARRY: I think you're right, Harry, people don't get it, and that's just the start, because once we've understood the customer's needs we then need to think about how we propose, how we present, how we get our message across. I always use proposals. I always put together that written document, which shows I understand the company, I understand their needs. I understand what I can do to help them. I've got to help them understand that I understand. I also explain a little about us as a company and then justify why we're pricing it the way we are, what they get out of it. I know that when I go into a presentation, I can do a really good job because I'm prepared.

HARRY: I know you do a good job; I've seen you do it. You're a class act. Your presentations have always got a structure. It's always beginning, middle and end. And it's very clear. You spike at the beginning, you get people engaged in what it is about and explain what you're going to say, you keep it animated and interesting. You keep people thinking through what it is that you're going to do for them and that's really good, Larry. I appreciate what you do.

LARRY: What else did we learn on that course? I'm just trying to think back now.

HARRY: Well, we learned how to be professionals, if you remember. We learned about how we plan, how we set ourselves up to manage what is basically our own business. We think about our area and we think about customers we need to go and speak to. We think about how we can maximise our time. Remember the guy who was talking about time management, and that really it is *self*-management? That it was important to appreciate that it's really about how we manage ourselves, focusing on the priority elements that would really make a difference? Considering urgent and important, wasn't it?

LARRY: Yeah. Self-management. It absolutely makes sense to me. I think I'm still pretty good at that sort of stuff. Can you remember the other training we went to that followed up? What was it, six months, a year after that?

HARRY: Oh yeah. Developing your sales experience. Didn't you let yourself down at that training as well?

LARRY: No, I didn't. That's a made-up story. I never did what everybody said. Let's just think about what it is that we learned.

HARRY: Well, I remember it really built on a lot of those essentials, but the thing that struck was that we that we spent a little bit more time on the psychology of selling. We learned about personality styles. We were recognising how different people respond to things in different ways, how they have preferences in the way that they think. And so, we can adapt what it is that we say and do.

LARRY: Yeah, it was a good session. I loved the sales psychology bit.

HARRY: And the fact we've got to tap into the emotions. That's an important part. I use that a lot today. I always try to think: what are these underlying motivators that people have and how can we make sure we're fulfilling those as well?

LARRY: I think it stood me in good stead.

HARRY: Well, you've been successful, right?

LARRY: I have. I think I've got an approach that really works. Next year it's head down and more of the same.

HARRY: Agreed. I'm going to have a little look at virtual and video selling, though. I think that's something that's developing.

LARRY: Really? Hmm. I'm not so sure.

HARRY: I think it is. A couple of people already started to ask me to talk to them on video conference. And, you know, using that technology seems to make sense to me. I don't know yet, but I'm going to go away and have a look; I'm going to try and bring it in because I want to keep developing.

LARRY: Yeah. Well, I'm not so sure. I think we've already got a good solid basis. I think we know a lot of good techniques and I reckon we've got to be able to get in front of customers, see the whites of their eyes and do the stuff that we do. We've got a way that works. Why change a winning formula?

HARRY: Okay. Well, I'm going to have a look. I'll let you know how I get on.

LARRY: Yeah. We ought to meet a bit more often than we do now.

HARRY: Yeah, let's try and do that earlier in the year.

And so that was how the conversation between Harry and Larry went; in December 2019, they departed the best of friends as before. All set up for a successful 2020.

2
Virtual Insanity

March 2020

What happened in 2020?

Well, as we know, 2020 was one hell of a year. There were some huge changes caused by a global pandemic. COVID-19 was responsible for some big shifts across many different industries, sales and the way we had to go about selling being one of them.

It is interesting for us to hear Harry and Larry's next conversation, a tense phone call in March.

HARRY: Hey Larry, how are you getting on? You sound a bit stressed.

LARRY: Well, of course I am stressed. Haven't you been hit by all this upheaval, all these changes? COVID is a nightmare. I cannot go and speak to any of my customers. I don't know what to do. I am a little bit panicky, to be honest, because I cannot really see the end of it.

HARRY: Um, yeah, I know, I am with you there. It is weird. It is hard, but I am just about doing OK.

LARRY: Really? Why, what are you doing? Please let me in on the secret here. Tell me, what are you doing that I should be thinking about too?

HARRY: Well, remember I said I was going to have a look at virtual selling? I have started to get my head around that. And I am really pleased I did, because as soon as we hit lockdown and customers were saying they didn't want to see us I was able to shift all my activity into being able to work online with them.

LARRY: Really? Oh, I am struggling because people are not seeing me, and I'm lost. I am trying to call people, but that is hard, as you know, I like to be in front of folk and I am finding it tough.

HARRY: Well you still can, if you think about it: by going virtual and using video conferencing tools, you are still in front of people.

LARRY: It's not the same though, is it?

HARRY: No, it is a bit different, but let's think about some of the things that we can do. You can still talk to people. You can still see them. You can still share information. Actually, I'm finding that I'm very, very efficient with this way of working because I can have more meetings now. People are also in a bit of a tailspin, so they need our help. I am booking meetings to talk to people about how we can help them now and how what we were doing before is probably going to be different as a result of all this change. I reassure them that we have got their backs and will look after them.

LARRY: OK. That is something that I need to understand a bit better. Can you give me a little bit more information on it?

HARRY: Of course I can. So, in short, because there is quite a lot to this, if you think about virtual selling as getting online with people and talking to them, using the technology that's available, that's the starting point. So, phones, like you said, are still very much a way of working. And you can still message. People are still sending and reading emails like before, but a lot of people are now doing more virtual conference calls.

LARRY: Yeah. I am not sure I like them. I don't really understand them.

HARRY: Well, let me see if I can make it easy for you. I think about the big five, as there are five things that…

if we can do these well, we can have a pretty good meeting online.

LARRY: What are these big five?

HARRY: So the big five, they are video, audio, having a decent background, good lighting and yourself.

LARRY: OK. Well, I need to know more, because I need to get my head around this.

HARRY: So, video. This is about how you use your camera, how you position your head, how you can look at it, how you make eye contact and how you can make sure that you are projecting the right image. You enhance your body language so people can read what it is you are trying to say, and you look at what they're doing and interpret that.

LARRY: So, a little bit like we do face to face.

HARRY: Exactly like we would do face to face, except you are doing it in front of a camera rather than sat across the table.

LARRY: Hmmm.

HARRY: Give it a go, Larry. It works. I would also suggest you make sure you get your audio right, though.

LARRY: So what do you mean by that?

HARRY: Well, you are going to be speaking on it and people have got to hear you well. If they cannot hear you, it's likely they will get frustrated because they won't be able to make sense of the stuff you're saying. In fact, in the training I took, they were talking about a study in Canada where they played the same audio to people, but they disrupted some of it. The people who heard the disrupted audio felt the person that they were speaking to was less credible.

LARRY: For real?

HARRY: Yeah. When you can't hear somebody, your brain has to work harder and you turn off your attention quicker.

LARRY: Yeah, that is true. I do find that.

HARRY: So I make sure I don't use the computer microphone.

LARRY: Yeah?

HARRY: I did use the headphones that came with my phone. But I just invested in a decent headset because I know the microphone on that will make me sound better. And I want customers to find it easier to listen to me. I don't want them to tune out.

LARRY: OK. So, I have got to look good on camera. And I have got to sound good.

HARRY: Yeah. That is pretty much it so far.

LARRY: Okey-dokey; what else do I need to know?

HARRY: Well, just think about how you are set up with your background. People are going to see where you are sat, or indeed where you are stood, but I'll talk about that in a minute. So just think about what is going on behind you. Is it going to look neat and tidy? Is it going to give a professional impression? Are you going to use, like your own natural background, or are you going to use a virtual background?

LARRY: What's a virtual background?

HARRY: It is a background the computer helps you generate, so you can put something behind you that is not real. And it just looks as though that is where you are sat.

LARRY: Oh, like the guy I spoke with the other day: it looked like he was in space.

HARRY: That's exactly it. I am not sure I would recommend sitting in space, as a salesperson. It just looks a little bit inappropriate.

LARRY: It was stupid. Yeah, it was funny, but to be honest I couldn't take him that seriously. So, what do you do?

HARRY: Me personally, I use natural background, and I just make sure it is tidy.

LARRY: Nothing too distracting.

HARRY: Exactly, don't have people walking about in the background. I also make sure that I have good lighting.

LARRY: Why do you need good lighting?

HARRY: Again, it goes back to what we were saying about video. People need to see you. People need to be able to read your facial expressions. I bought a ring light, didn't cost me much but it helps people see my face. I also make sure that if I am sat with the window to one side that it's not causing too much brightness on one side of my face compared to the other.

LARRY: You're really thinking about this stuff, aren't you?

HARRY: I am, because it makes a difference; and they are only little things, but they do start to stack up. Anyway, think about it. This is how we need to operate these days. This is how we are talking to our customers now. If you are going out to a customer, you'd make sure your shoes were shined and that you looked smart.

LARRY: Of course, goes without saying.

HARRY: It is the virtual equivalent. That is what we are trying to do, right?

LARRY: Yeah, it makes sense.

HARRY: When I first started it I was probably a little bit like you in that I wasn't sure it would work. However, I have seen that it does. And so, I do treat these as proper meetings. It's the same as if I had got in a car, driven two hours and gone and seen the customer except the bonus is, I've not driven two hours. I can have more of these meetings.

LARRY: So what else can you teach me?

HARRY: Right. Well as I think of these as important meetings, I do the same drills as I would if it were in person. You know, I'll send the agenda, I'll dress properly, I'll prepare and be ready to do the stuff that we do as professional salespeople.

LARRY: I don't know.

HARRY: Look, I can tell you what I do. I can tell you what is working. I can only encourage you to go and try, because I cannot see the end of this.

LARRY: We'll be out and about soon. It won't be too bad.

HARRY: I am not so sure. And anyway, I am wondering whether the customers are going to find that they like this. I am already hearing some customers saying they are finding this a cool way of collaborating.

LARRY: Nah, how can they say that you can collaborate properly? How would you get around the table or use a whiteboard?

HARRY: Well, you can use whiteboards online, you know. You can do several things to create a similar experience. I often just open a blank PowerPoint slide and then I just type on that with that screen being shared, so people can see what it is that we are saying, to keep a track of it. I will bullet the main points of the meeting. Sometimes I will use the pen and annotate things. I draw on my screen and people can see what I'm drawing.

LARRY: Oh, I've seen that; it looks a little bit messy.

HARRY: It might look a bit messy, but it's effective. Remember, people are visual animals. If they can see stuff, it will help them understand better.

LARRY: I guess.

HARRY: That is just the way I do it. There are other things available. I mean, I've started having a bit of a play with more formal online whiteboards. These you can open and share with anybody. I am starting to send people to a link to the whiteboard, so they can draw on it at the same time.

LARRY: Now you're losing me.

HARRY: So, I will send a link to the virtual whiteboard. We will both have it open and write on it. What we are writing will come up at the same time on both my screen and their screen.

LARRY: That sounds like when you are stood with the customer in front of the whiteboard, we've both got a pen in our hands and we're writing stuff.

HARRY: That's exactly what we're doing, and we can then take a screenshot or we can save it. We can even use it in between the meetings to keep the job moving.

LARRY: Wow. This sounds a bit complicated, though.

HARRY: Don't make it complicated. Don't run before you can walk. Just go and think about how you can get better at just talking into a camera. It's just talking to people and you are good at that, Larry. We are professional salespeople. We are not taking that away. All the stuff we were talking about last time, that is still very much in play. We are just bringing in another dimension, about how we need to do that.

LARRY: It sounds as though you are really developing a lot in this area. I bet you're doing other things as well, knowing you.

HARRY: As a matter of fact, I am. I've come across this concept of synchronous and asynchronous communication.

LARRY: Now you are talking psychobabble.

HARRY: [*Laughs*] Not really. It just about the stuff that we might do in a meeting. And then the stuff that we are doing between meetings, think of it like that.

LARRY: Um, yeah, OK.

HARRY: Think about it. What would we do in a meeting? We would discuss something. We would ask people questions and might want to get answers once we are out of the meeting, so we would get in touch. We would send a follow-up. We would put together a document to help people understand what it is that we talked about and to keep the whole sale moving forward.

LARRY: Yeah, that *is* right.

HARRY: Well, that's not changed. But rather than just use the document, we can use video.

LARRY: Like, just record a video and send it?

HARRY: Exactly that. You can do that on your phone. You have got a studio in your pocket, so you could just talk to your phone camera, save the video and send it to people. There are other ways in which you can use that technology to make that easier for you. But that is something that works well. Customers like it.

LARRY: How would you know?

HARRY: They tell me. Honestly, I have sent videos and they told me they like it. I sent videos to people that I didn't know and when I eventually talked to them they told me they felt as though they were starting to know me already, before I'd even met them. I was starting to build the relationship really early. Think about it. You see somebody, you look at their face, you start to read them and process whether they are friend or foe. If you are saying something about… because you have done your research, they will warm to you quicker. We can use technology to be more human. Technology doesn't dehumanise selling if we use it properly.

LARRY: Wow, my head is starting to spin a little bit!

HARRY: Maybe, but it is something that I would really encourage you to take on board. It is something that you will find useful in keeping modern and keeping in contact with the customers, that I know you serve well.

LARRY: Well, I am not sure I do at the moment, as I'm not really talking to them.

HARRY: Exactly. Get yourself in front of them. Set up a video call, use Teams, use Zoom, use WebEx, use whatever, even FaceTime them, do something that just helps you keep in front of them and keep the conversations going, because I know you do a good job, Larry. I know you do.

LARRY: Well, there is a lot of stuff to think about.

HARRY: Larry, you are a good salesperson, you just need to adapt a little. Give it a go; I'm here to help if you need it.

That is how the friends finished their conversation, trying to make sense in a confusing world.

3
Opportunity Knocks

May 2020

We join Harry and Larry in May 2020.

Harry was pleased that Larry set up a video call, but a was a bit shocked to see his friend looking tired and stressed.

HARRY: Larry, how are you doing? How you are getting on?

LARRY: Struggling.

HARRY: For real? Why, what's up?

LARRY: Well, I'm still not seeing customers. It's still hard. I still can't go and visit them. I still can't work my magic. You know how I like to work with them.

HARRY: I do. But the kind of the stuff we talked about last time, haven't you done any of that?

LARRY: Uh, yeah, I tried a couple of video calls, but they were not so good. I did a little bit on LinkedIn, too.

HARRY: Remember, I never said it was easy. When you said you did a little bit on LinkedIn, what do you do?

LARRY: I changed my profile and… and that's it.

HARRY: Did you do any posts, did you put anything up on there?

LARRY: Like what?

HARRY: Well, like interesting information for customers about things that you are doing. Stuff that they might find helpful in the current climate, about yourself, anything that people can look at and learn a little bit more about you from.

LARRY: I've not done anything like that.

HARRY: Well how are you expecting it to work? It is about putting things out there that people will find interesting. People will be able to look at what you are up to and recognise they need to do something similar. I am using it quite a lot now and I'm getting some decent reactions and having conversations as a result. And, to be honest, it has opened up a couple of opportunities.

LARRY: How?

HARRY: I would say it is early days, but at least we are starting some discussions. I am concentrating on trying to put something valuable out at least once a day, so I look like someone people want to talk to.

LARRY: Hmm. OK. But how do you know what to say?

HARRY: Just look around, look around at what's going on. You can find so much that could be valuable. Think of when you have had a conversation with a customer. What was it that they were asking you? How did you answer them? Look at what other people are posting. Don't copy them, but you can certainly think, well, if that's what people are posting, that seems to be what people are interested in.

LARRY: I'm a bit worried about doing that... worried about, well, putting myself out there.

HARRY: But that's our job. We are salespeople. That's what we do. We need to be connecting and talking to people. This is another way in which we can connect, and we need to be connecting and talking and influencing as many people as possible.

LARRY: Well, I suppose I can't really argue that.

HARRY: No, you can't, because it's true. I've also been doing a little bit more work around learning things that can help me to sell better.

LARRY: You don't stop trying to learn stuff, do you?

HARRY: [*Laughs*] But why should I, when it's our job to keep developing? It's our job to keep getting better, to keep pushing forward.

LARRY: So what have you learned now?

HARRY: Well, my latest thing is opportunity management.

LARRY: Go on.

HARRY: So opportunity management is fundamentally about understanding how people make decisions and what's important to them.

LARRY: Hasn't it always been that?

HARRY: Yes, it has. But what I'm finding is, I don't think we've been going deep enough.

LARRY: Well, we've been doing this gig ten years. It's always been good enough before.

HARRY: Remember: stuff is changing, and changing at pace. So, we really need to be thinking about how we can start to understand people involved in the buying decision and answering certain questions. Things like: how do they make those decisions? What are they thinking? What's important to them? What challenges do they have? What issues? What concerns? What goals have they got, or aspirations do they have?

LARRY: That's a lot of stuff to think about.

HARRY: It *is* a lot of stuff, but that's how we need to be selling. We need to get as deep as possible with them… provide relevant information that's going to help them with all those things. And we've got to do it for a lot of people.

LARRY: Yeah. I usually try to speak to a couple of people from each company.

HARRY: I reckon you're probably not speaking to enough.

LARRY: How can you say that?

HARRY: Quite easily, really. I base it on research. One of the things that we've seen from some research coming out recently is that, whereas a couple of years ago we probably needed to speak to five or six people, that went up last year to about eight. Now it is seeming that on average we should be speaking to around twelve people. And I know, with our kind of sale, that's about right.

LARRY: That many?

HARRY: Just think about it. All those people who are now wanting to get involved in having a say in what we do.

LARRY: I guess you're right; I am not speaking to that many.

HARRY: This has really opened my eyes. And so, I have started to take a far more structured approach in how I work on each opportunity, and how I manage it. I've started to really understand the discipline of opportunity management.

LARRY: Go on.

HARRY: Well, opportunity management is different from activity management, which you would know about, as that is putting stuff in your sales pipeline.

LARRY: Yep.

HARRY: Not all the stuff that goes in the top comes out at the bottom. So, we need to find a good level of activity to keep on top of things and give ourselves the best chance of winning the opportunities we are presented with. Think of it a bit like account management but slightly different.

LARRY: How?

HARRY: Account management is the overall account plan. It's what we're doing in the grand scheme of things. And that needs certain skills. But opportunity management is specifically about looking at a certain project or certain opportunities. It's taking a chance we've got to sell and managing that through a certain thinking process to be able to get to the point that we can close, negotiate and win the deal.

LARRY: So selling then?

HARRY: Absolutely it's selling, but as selling is becoming more complex, we need to think about what we can do to understand all those different dynamics and keep track of what's going on.

LARRY: So how would you do that, then?

HARRY: Well, I've found something which is pretty cool, and simplified the whole thing for me. There are nine boxes of information that we need to understand.

LARRY: Go on then, talk me through these nine boxes. What do I need to know?

HARRY: Let's start off at a high level. There are three key things we need to understand. It's all about information. So, we have got to get some data. We talked about the number of people involved, so now we've got to understand the DMU, the decision-making unit. And then we've got to think about what decisions *we* are going to make. What actions do we have to put in place?

LARRY: Well, that's selling.

HARRY: Again, you're right. We're not doing anything different here, but what this does, it really makes us think about things in a certain way. So, when we look at the basic data, what we're doing is, we're thinking about who's the account and what's the opportunity? Does the opportunity make sense for us? We've got to qualify it.

LARRY: Qualify out!

HARRY: Yeah, qualify out. If it doesn't make a lot of sense for us to work on a project we need to stop. It's not something that we are necessarily very good at. So you're right, qualify out.

LARRY: I do find that pretty hard.

HARRY: We all find it hard. It kind of goes against the grain as a salesperson. But if we can be quite objective about it, if we know the criteria that we need to look at, we can make that decision far easier for ourselves. We can base it on the things that we know make a difference with the kind of opportunity that we are looking for.

LARRY: OK. So, we pick the right opportunity. What do we do next?

HARRY: I then like to think about the competition. We can think about who we're selling against, including the 'do nothing' option. We might well have competitors that are also going to try with that business, so we need to think about: what's our position?

LARRY: What do you mean by 'position'?

HARRY: How likely are we to win this business? From hot to cold. I like the concept of a thermometer and doing a temperature check as an indicator of how well I'm doing.

LARRY: OK. And what do you base that on?

HARRY: Well, I'll partly base that on the people involved. I'll base that on the DMU. You know about that, we've done this before, haven't we? You know how we've mapped out all the people who have a say on the deal?

LARRY: Oh yeah. I remember this stuff. I still do it. Who are they? What's their name? What's the job? And what role do they play in making the decision?

HARRY: Yeah. Go on, Larry.

LARRY: The role was about whether they were users or whether they were basing a decision on criteria.

HARRY: Yep. That's right. Technical criteria or commercial criteria.

LARRY: Yeah, there it was. The big decision maker. What did we call that?

HARRY: We call that the economic buyer as we did not want to call it decision maker because then it takes away from the focus on the whole DMU.

LARRY: Yeah. Got it.

HARRY: And the coach. Remember, the person who's going to help us.

LARRY: Yeah. That's right. What else did we talk about? Let me think. Ah yes, we talked about understanding what their needs were? What is it they're trying to achieve? What wants did they have? What would be a win for them? What are we trying to satisfy and how would we exceed expectations?

HARRY: Yep, absolutely. That's what we're looking at. And then remember we were looking at the kind of the influence that they had on the decision. Whether they were with us or against us, and how strong their influence was, you know, whether people really listened to them or not.

LARRY: So, what's new then?

HARRY: Well, I'm getting far more disciplined at doing all that. I take the information and I process it far better. I will start to look at the actions I've got to take as a result of what I know. For instance, I know if I'm missing information, then I need to find that out.

LARRY: Hmmm, interesting.

HARRY: So we summarise that into the boxes. I then look and go, right, what would be possible actions? What could I do because of this? And from the possible actions, I look at it from a reality perspective and decide what are the best actions that are going to give me a good bang for my buck. Have most impact. I ask myself, how can I make it work? And that gives me a clear plan of what I'm doing with every opportunity. How I need to move it forward and how I can work better, because I'm clearer in my thinking.

LARRY: But that's why I kind of do anyway.

HARRY: Listen to what you just said.

LARRY: What did I just say?

HARRY: You said 'kind of do anyway'.

LARRY: Yeah, I do kind of do it.

HARRY: Well, the point is to be less kind of and far more deliberate in the stuff that we're doing, because then we know that's going to really make a difference.

LARRY: Well, I can see that. I guess it just sounds like a lot of work.

HARRY: It *is* a lot of work, but it's our job and we get out what we put in. You know, if I put in the work, if I understand this stuff, if I can spot areas in which I can help someone, if I can work with somebody, do something I've not done, or find out about something that somebody else is doing better and I need to work against, I can be far more effective in my sales job. This is what modern selling is really coming down to. We need to be structured and thoughtful in how we're going to influence all the people that are involved in these decisions.

LARRY: Well, that's difficult for me to argue against, but I think it's what I just do naturally.

HARRY: That's what I felt. And of course, we *have* been successful. But when you start to map it, you see the things that you're not doing. Also, remember, a lot of the things that people were looking for have changed now. And if we're not careful and approaching things with our old perspectives rather than what is it they need, what is it they want, their key issues and priorities here and now in this current climate, how can we add value? I'll be very deliberate in keeping track of that and making sure that I'm doing the best job possible for my customers.

LARRY: Hmm, makes sense. Every time I see you, I feel as if I'm leaving with homework.

HARRY: Well, I'm not a teacher, and you aren't a schoolboy. You're a professional salesperson. Structure is there to help you do that.

LARRY: I understand. It just feels terribly overwhelming. This is a lot of stuff to do here. It's hard, you know, it's hard.

HARRY: I didn't say it was easy, but I'm here to help, Larry, and I'm happy to share. I want you to succeed. I want you to move forward and yeah, when we next chat, I want to see that smile back on your face.

LARRY: Well, I don't feel like smiling so much.

HARRY: Just try to control the controllable. Do the stuff so that you can have a better understanding of things and you will feel in a far better place. Trust me, this is what I'm doing. That's how I'm staying so upbeat. It's really helping.

LARRY: I'm pleased for you. Bit envious, really.

HARRY: You might be. But you can do this too. It works. I promise you.

That is how Harry and Larry's discussion went. It seems that, as we moved into the middle of the year, Harry was doing far better than Larry. He was adopting new thinking. He was open to new ways of working. He was keeping a positive mindset. He was pushing himself out of his comfort zone. Larry, not so much. You can hear his struggles. He is finding it quite tough.

4

Leading The Way

June 2020

As we get into the middle of the year, it seems that Harry is doing far better than Larry. He is adopting new thinking and is open to new ways of working. He is keeping a positive mindset and pushing himself out of his comfort zone. Larry, not so much. As you will hear, he is struggling and finding things quite tough. Let's listen in to their next meeting.

HARRY: Hey, Larry. How are you doing?

LARRY: Honestly, not so good.

HARRY: Really? Tell me about it.

LARRY: It's just all the stuff that's going on. I was waiting until I could get back out and do the stuff I used to, but I can't see when that's going to happen. Lockdowns don't seem to finish, customers don't want to go back to doing what they used to do. Everything is different.

HARRY: Everything *is* different. Did you try any of the things I suggested?

LARRY: I've done a bit.

HARRY: Well, OK. I am going to be quite direct to you, Larry, because I've got your best interest in heart. If you only do a bit, you'll only get a bit back. What I've done is really throw myself out there. I've worked hard, but I'm reaping the rewards. I'm talking to people, I'm getting results. Customers are coming to me now. I'm not having to force myself on them. They want to interact. Look, I'm not saying this to rub your nose in it; it's because these are the facts and I want you to be in the same position.

LARRY: I *want* to be in the same position.

HARRY: You've got to do new stuff, then. You know I'm learning law stuff?

LARRY: You and your learning.

HARRY: Yeah, because it makes a difference. The more that I can learn, the better, because I can apply it and I can help my customers. That's what I'm finding now.

LARRY: Is that the latest lesson?

HARRY: If you want to treat it like that.

LARRY: I might as well.

HARRY: OK, here's the latest lesson, then. I've become more and more aware that we're change agents. We're trying to get customers to change. That's what we've always done in sales. We're trying to move people. We're trying to influence them. We're trying to do this for their own good.

LARRY: Yeah. That's fair.

HARRY: Very much so. Our skills as change agents are key. That's what we've got to do. Customers are often stuck.

LARRY: Customers are stuck? I'm stuck!

HARRY: That's why I am trying to practise what I preach. And I'm talking to you because I want you to be able to use this stuff to help other people.

LARRY: I *want* to help other people.

HARRY: I know you do. So, think of yourself as a change agent. Think about how you can understand them, their issues, their concerns, and how you can help them move through their change curve. Remember the work we did a little bit back, where we learned that people deal with change in different ways and that if we can recognise where they are in that process, we can adapt how we work with them so that we're doing what's right for them at the time?

LARRY: I kind of remember.

HARRY: Well, think about it like this. I know that I see change as an opportunity. I relish it and I'll try and implement things to take advantage of the fact that things are different. It gives me an opportunity to talk to people and show them new things. However, I know I've got to be careful; when people are being affected by change, they might be in denial. Or they might be getting quite angry about the situation, quite frustrated, quite confused. I can overwhelm them with being too excited, too positive. So, I sometimes must temper what I do.

LARRY: We should do that with me.

HARRY: I *am* doing it with you. I've played this right down, but I'm going to be more direct with you because I know that is what you want. I've known you for a long time and I know that if I can give your cage a bit of a rattle you'll come through.

LARRY: Yeah. Fair enough. I know I can be a bit negative sometimes.

HARRY: Not normally. But I've seen you over the last few months, when you *have* been a bit negative, and I know that it's not you. Which is why I want to help you. I want to help you, just like I would help my customers.

LARRY: Nah, it *is* appreciated. It's just hard.

HARRY: I totally understand; and I'm not saying it's easier for me. It's just that I'm trying to embrace it and I'm trying to learn. The whole scenario is confusing, but I've come across this really cool model that I'm using to try and get my own head around things and which I'm sharing with customers.

LARRY: You and your models.

HARRY: Because they work, to help understand and make sense of a situation so that we can then explain it a bit better and then use our skills as salespeople to help customers out.

LARRY: Fair enough. So, what are you going to share with me?

HARRY: VUCA.

LARRY: No need to be rude!

HARRY: *[Laughs]* No, VUCA: V – U – C – A.

LARRY: What is VUCA when it's at home?

HARRY: VUCA's a model that was originally used by the military. At the end of the Cold War things got a little bit confusing because it wasn't clear who the enemy was, any more. Military and security forces had to adapt and what they said is that the conditions they found themselves in were VUCA, which stands for volatile, uncertain, complex and ambiguous.

LARRY: Say those again?

HARRY: Volatile, uncertain, complex and ambiguous; or volatility, uncertainty, complexity and ambiguity.

LARRY: OK, got ya.

HARRY: And that pretty much describes the situation we're in at the moment, right?

LARRY: It does.

HARRY: Well, in 2007 a guy called Bob Johansen came up with the VUCA Prime model as a way in which we can deal with those kinds of situations.[1] How we can sort of neutralise them, if you like. There are ways that we in the business world can do stuff to take those away, or to minimise the threats that they might bring.

LARRY: OK. Tell me more.

HARRY: Well, it's pretty cool because it uses the same initials. It is still VUCA. But what we are saying is that vision rises above volatility. Understanding reduces uncertainty. Clarity counters complexity, and agility overcomes ambiguity.

LARRY: Run them by me again. I will think I am with you.

HARRY: No problem. So, vision rises above volatility. That is what we want to do with customers anyway, we want to have a joint vision. We want to share what it is we're trying to achieve together. We can then form a plan and we can work on that. Things that we're doing become a lot more predictable, so we reduce volatility. Then, the better we can help customers understand where they want to be and how we can help them, the better we can work with them to achieve that. We can collaborate more with them.

LARRY: Totally. Yeah.

HARRY: OK. So, next up: understanding reduces uncertainty. If you think about it, uncertainty basically comes from not knowing stuff. The more we know, the easier it is to understand things. It's kind of obvious, really.

LARRY: Yeah. I guess it is.

HARRY: That's why we ask customers questions. Not necessarily so we get to know stuff, but by asking them questions, they can start to understand things better. We share information, we bring stuff to the table. We bring insight; remember, insight is the salesperson's most valuable commodity. We bring that so that people can start to get a better understanding of things. We help get rid of some of the unknown elements. And that's even if we're just uncovering the known unknowns by recognising what we don't know, and that we're going to do something about it.

LARRY: That's helpful. It makes sense. And I could see myself doing that.

HARRY: Cool. Well, I'm glad I'm getting a bit of clarity, because that's the whole point. Clarity counters complexity. We are in a complex situation now and there is much confusion going on. But the more that we can use things to help us become clear ourselves, and help the customer become clear in what they want to do, then the better we can operate as salespeople. That's why I like models. That's why I like processes. That's why I like having things that I can hang work and deliberate action around because it makes us far more effective.

LARRY: Yeah, you do love your models. To be fair, I can see that it works for you.

HARRY: Works for me, works for everyone, really. That's why I'm such a big fan.

LARRY: OK. What else do I need to know?

HARRY: Well, the last one is agility overcomes ambiguity. We want to be agile. We want to be able to react quickly. We need to respond to people. We've got to be able to say, look this has changed, this is different, this is a threat and this is something we need to deal with, but we're set up to do it. The more agile we become the more effective we can be. The better we can operate.

LARRY: Oh man, that *is* cool. I like VUCA.

HARRY: Absolutely. Understand VUCA and combat it with VUCA Prime. Try and think about how you can do that, because really it's good selling anyway. But if we're doing it very deliberately, if we're doing it very thoughtfully, it's the same as a lot of things we do as a salesperson, we can become better, more useful and add more value to customers.

LARRY: Yeah. I like it a lot.

HARRY: Cool. You look a little bit happier.

LARRY: Happier; not happy, but happier.

HARRY: Come on. You've got to be happy. You're understanding VUCA now. How cool is that?

LARRY: Yeah, pretty cool.

HARRY: So, are you going to do anything with it?

LARRY: I'm going to try.

HARRY: Come on. There is no try. Only do.

LARRY: OK, Yoda.

HARRY: *[Laughs]* I am your mentor. I will be your guide.

LARRY: Funny guy.

HARRY: Is it something that you can do, though?

LARRY: Yeah, I'm going to give it a go.

HARRY: May the force be with you.

The friends signed off their call, and though Harry was still concerned for Larry he knew him well enough to know he would be able to make sense of it all. From past experience he knew Larry was resilient and would be able to overcome these issues. He hoped that his friend would be able to do this sooner rather than later. In the meantime, Harry had plenty of thinking of his own to do.

5
Providing Valuable Insight

August 2020

Once again, Harry arranged to speak to Larry. Harry was a bit worried, as he had never seen his friend Larry so down. However, he was doing his bit, he was trying to share things to help his friend. Larry was certainly feeling overwhelmed and was not the only person to be experiencing that. It was an interesting journey for them, one that continued when they spoke next and the conversation turned to value selling.

LARRY: OK. I am sitting comfortably. What's my next lesson?

HARRY: Well, hello to you too! Not seen you for a couple of months. I'd like to know how you're getting on.

LARRY: Uh, I'm getting on.

HARRY: What does that even mean?

LARRY: I'm doing some of the stuff, like you said. It's making a little bit more sense. I tend to get a bit confused, though. I *do* still get disheartened. That said, I think there's a light at the end of the tunnel.

HARRY: There *is* a light at the end of the tunnel. If you're seeing this situation for the opportunity it is, and you're talking to customers and you're helping them, then absolutely, you *can* make a difference.

LARRY: Yeah. I make a bit of a difference.

HARRY: Oh, go on. Tell me how you've made a difference recently.

LARRY: I've started getting my head around virtual selling.

HARRY: Oh, cool. Go on. What have you been doing?

LARRY: Well, I've started booking more meetings. I realised this is how we need to operate. I realised that customers like it and I shouldn't have worried that they did not. What they're saying is, yeah, we're comfortable, we do this stuff and it's making us more effective. I recognise it's actually making me more effective, too.

HARRY: That's great. That really is great. So, what wins have you had recently?

LARRY: Well, I was talking to a customer and they said, at the end of the call, that it was great, that it was a valuable meeting.

HARRY: Boom! That's what you're about. That's the old Larry: customers love talking to you because you understand value.

LARRY: I don't understand value.

HARRY: You do. You're really good at understanding value.

LARRY: I disagree that I understand what value is; I'll tell you why.

HARRY: Go on, then.

LARRY: Value is a mystery.

HARRY: Yeah. I remember that training. That was so cool. When the guy asked 'What is value?' And we all tried to tell him what it is, and he said, 'Well, how can you even say that? Because value is a mystery'; and we all said, 'What do you mean?' He went on to explain that it depends on what the customer thinks it is. We've got to find that out, our job is to find out what they think value is and then show that we can deliver on that. So, value is a mystery. Yeah. I remember, it just made me think of Scooby Doo.

LARRY: What?

HARRY: 'Value is a mystery' made me think about the old Scooby Doo van.

LARRY: Excuse me?

HARRY: The Scooby Doo van was called the Mystery Machine.

LARRY: Harry, you need to get out more.

HARRY: I always thought Scooby Doo stories were a bit like selling value. They had to find out who done it, which was usually the janitor. I think that's a little bit like what we do, selling value.

LARRY: How can Scooby Doo and the janitor be about value selling?

HARRY: Well, they investigate, they understand. They try to work out, with the clues that they've got, who it is. They have a reasonable idea who it would be, as it's always the janitor. But they never actually accuse him until they find out properly and use the proof. Well, I think that's a bit like value selling.

LARRY: Yeah, I suppose it is. So, is that how you sell value, then? You rock up and pretend you're Scooby Doo?

HARRY: *[Laughs]* No; I'm a bit more structured than that.

LARRY: Oh yeah, of course, structures.

HARRY: Of course; as structures are designed to give us a game plan to do things that help us work more effectively.

LARRY: So what is your structure for selling value?

HARRY: Same as yours. Can you remember the training?

LARRY: Uh, more or less. It's pretty much what you said and that is, find out what value and communicate it.

HARRY: True. But if we just break that down a little bit further, we can do a slightly better job. We are trained to understand what value is for the customer. We work that out with them so that they recognise value for themselves. But how people perceive value is always changing. That for me is really important now, because of all the changes that are going on. I've found that there are many accounts I'm working with where I had understood pretty well with them what value was, but that what's important to them now has changed massively.

LARRY: You're right. We can be talking about one thing and suddenly the conversation has gone to something completely different.

HARRY: It's our job to understand that and how it's changing for different people. We talked about mapping DMUs before. How are you getting on with that?

LARRY: I've become a bit more disciplined; and you're right, the more I dig into things, the more I realise that there are probably more people than those I'm currently speaking to who need to be involved.

HARRY: Well, that's a great thing.

LARRY: Yeah. But it *is* a bit disheartening.

HARRY: No, not disheartening at all. Because when you understand that, you can do something about it. You identify who they are. And then, when you understand what's important to them, that's when you can differentiate. Remember what the guy said about differentiation on the course?

LARRY: Yeah. Being different is not a differentiator.

HARRY: Bang on. And that stuck with me. 'Cause I remember saying to a customer once, 'Oh, we are different to other suppliers'. The customer pretty much said to me 'I don't care'. When she told me that I realised that it really is our job to understand what matters to them and are we different in a way relevant to them? Can we package our stuff accordingly so that it then sets us apart?

LARRY: And communicate it...

HARRY: Absolutely; communicate it. Do a really good job and position that value so that they understand it. And make sure, then, that they appreciate that, because we're going to have to put a price to it. We're not in business just for the fun of it. It's not as though we're a charity.

LARRY: Yeah. There's a lot of pushback now. People saying that they're finding it tricky and that we need to reduce prices and we need to do all sorts of discounting and special deals.

HARRY: And how are you dealing with those conversations?

LARRY: Not so well.

HARRY: So for me that comes back to value selling. We know what value is for them, we've captured it and we've priced it, aligned to that. Basically, we're offering what they need to buy to be able to do what they want to achieve. It should be a win–win situation.

LARRY: Mutual benefit.

HARRY: We need to explain that so that they understand that's why the price is what it is. We've got to be in this for mutual benefit. This is what you'll get from it and this is what we need to work together. So yeah, we need to benefit from the deal, too, and that's usually financial. But then we're going to make sure that we deliver on it. That for me is the structure of how we go through understanding, communicating and delivering on value. I think it boils down to that.

LARRY: It does. But it doesn't get any easier.

HARRY: Who said sales was an easy life?

LARRY: I know. It's just really hard at the moment.

HARRY: But remember, it's hard for everyone. If we can make it easier for people that can be part of our value. That could be the mystery.

LARRY: Yes. If we understand that could fit well with mystery solving. Why don't we sell on that?

HARRY: It's something that we *can* do. It's something that we can very much play on as one of our strengths.

LARRY: Yeah, I guess you're right.

HARRY: It's always going to be hard work. We've got to work hard. I'm working hard, you're working hard. But we've got to work smart, too.

LARRY: So true. I feel a bit more confident about what we should be doing.

HARRY: You're good at this.

LARRY: Yeah, I am.

HARRY: You are. So tell me again.

LARRY: I'm good at this.

HARRY: Right. So, get out there and start having those conversations that you had before with customers about how you can deliver value for them. Just use all the different tools, technologies, ways of thinking that you've got at your fingertips to be of value yourself. Your conversations in themselves can be valuable. The buying experience, how they work with Larry is something that should start to set you apart. You can do it.

LARRY: I can do it.

HARRY: Do you want to look more convinced, then?

LARRY: Yeah. OK. I *am* convinced.

It was a shorter conversation than those before but no less valuable. Larry did leave looking a bit more chipper, though Harry was still worried about his old buddy. However, he could see that Larry was beginning to move to the way of selling that Harry himself was finding more effective, and finding successful. He did not always want to say this to Larry, because he felt a bit guilty at succeeding where his friend was still struggling. However, it did make him able to share what was making a difference, able to move his friend along, so that Larry could be successful too.

6
Expansion Plans

October 2020

Let's join Harry and Larry in their next discussion.

HARRY: Hi Larry. How are you doing?

LARRY: All right. Are you going to get all deep again on me in this conversation? Only joking, I appreciate it really. How are you?

HARRY: I'm good, as always. Funnily enough, I was thinking about our last discussion as I sometimes feel a bit guilty because it's going all right for me. I'm interested in hearing how it is going for you, though.

LARRY: Slightly better than it was before.

HARRY: Well, that's good to hear.

LARRY: It *is* better because it was terrible before.

HARRY: Oh come on, you've been doing OK, you must be doing all right as you've always been successful.

LARRY: Yeah, I have been and thankfully I'm still making sales to customers. I *am* getting bit more comfortable with it all.

HARRY: That's great. I like it. So, what are you up to now?

LARRY: Well, I'm starting to get to a position with some projects where I'm having feedback calls.

HARRY: Brilliant stuff. That's brilliant.

LARRY: Yeah. I took on some of the things you were saying. I think I can still do them better, but it has opened up some opportunities which we're starting to deliver on and now I want to find out whether people are getting the value we promised.

HARRY: How can you do that?

LARRY: Well, I'm just going to schedule a call.

HARRY: Will it be a video call or phone call?

LARRY: Uh, probably video, because I want to read the reactions.

HARRY: Good answer.

LARRY: I'm going to arrange a call and I'm just going to pretty much ask them directly, 'Are you getting value out of the project that we are working on?'

HARRY: Closed question. Why is that?

LARRY: Well, I pretty much want a yes or no answer. If they are, I'm going to say that's brilliant and ask about becoming a case study. I'll also see if there's anyone else that would benefit from something similar, from what I am working with them on.

HARRY: Go for it. What if they say no?

LARRY: Well, I'm going to say sorry. Because I will be sorry. But I'll then want to dig deep and to understand why not. Though I might be a bit more careful with phrasing the question.

HARRY: How do you mean?

LARRY: Well, people can become a bit defensive. So, I might well ask one of the TED questions we learned back in the day.

HARRY: Oh yeah. TED questions. Tell me, explain, describe.

LARRY: Spot on, same as a why really.

HARRY: What are you expecting they will say?

LARRY: They will give me more detail so that I can understand what is or isn't happening, and then I can do something about it. I can then offer a way of making sure they get the value we promised, for which I'll bear the complete cost.

HARRY: You have to sort it.

LARRY: What I've found in the past is that, as well as offering to deal with it, sometimes it also makes sense to discuss enhancing the whole offer, too. They need to pay for that option but it can be the right thing for us to do, as things have changed and that is a better way to work now. But I would never give only that option, I've got to offer to fix it for free.

HARRY: Sounds like you've got this stuff nailed.

LARRY: I've always been good at this. Like we were saying last year, when I was doing well was partly because I was having these calls and I was getting a lot of goodwill out of them, you know, people were happy. They would often start to talk about more business. I would never lead it. I don't like to do that because if I'm saying it's a feedback call, I don't want them to think it's a disguised sales call. That said, if they want to speak about other projects, happy days.

HARRY: Sounds like you really have got these calls sorted.

LARRY: Yeah. I just, I just wish there were more of them at the moment.

HARRY: There will be, because you're starting to have more conversations, and it sounds as if you use some of these techniques that we were talking about.

LARRY: I do. So what else are you going to teach me next?

HARRY: Nothing, really, that you don't already know.

LARRY: To be fair, when you remind me of things it is like learning.

HARRY: I know what you mean. Well, how about keeping in touch very deliberately? Every time you see something you think might be interesting to a person, share it with them. Send an email, pick up the phone, set a meeting. Whichever way you choose, you want to get it across to them.

LARRY: Mmmmm.

HARRY: I'm starting to blend things a little bit. So, I might find an article and I send the email, but I make a video of why I think it is useful for them and put that into the email. There are so many things that we can do to be a bit more creative in keeping in touch with folk and it does make a difference.

LARRY: Yeah. I like that blended idea.

HARRY: The whole point now is about blending. This is exactly what we've been talking about the last few months.

LARRY: Is it?

HARRY: Hybrid selling. That is basically what we've been discussing. It's a mixture of all the things that we've known before plus some newer thinking. We have tools. We have techniques. We have all these things that we can use to work better for our customers.

LARRY: Lots of different things are involved.

HARRY: Yeah, totally. So, it's a hybrid approach. Selling now is about having all these things so that we pick the ones that enable us to be most effective.

LARRY: Hybrid selling, eh? And we covered all the elements?

HARRY: I'd say we've touched on most things, but there is another I would add in, to give us a more complete approach, which is account management.

LARRY: Didn't we speak about that before, a couple months ago?

HARRY: No, we spoke about opportunity management, if you remember.

LARRY: Oh yeah. But isn't it the same thing?

HARRY: It's different. So, account management, this is that kind of bigger picture stuff where we're working with the account as a whole. We're working with the customer and we're making sure we're doing the things that will really cement that relationship, to make sure that we can maximise the benefits that we both get. Again, that needs certain skills, some of which are like sales, but some of which are slightly different.

LARRY: Well, how are they different?

HARRY: I'm not saying totally different. It is kind of the same but different. The ones that spring to mind are that the communication has got to be brilliant. As an account manager you'll probably need to communicate at lots of different levels, with lots of different people. You've got to be in touch with many different stakeholders. And we're talking both inside the account and within our own organisation.

LARRY: Yeah, makes sense. Agree on that one.

HARRY: I think we've also got to be expert in what our company does and what the customer does so that we can then really put a tailored offer together that aligns those goals. Ensure that we're working together towards mutual benefit.

LARRY: Like the stuff we learned about collaborative sales.

HARRY: That's right. We need a more strategic perspective. I think, for account managers, the goals tend to be a little bit longer-term rather than kind of just chasing the short-term sales figures. The focus would tend to be on what we're trying to do with them at a broader business level.

LARRY: Yeah. Again, I agree with you on that one.

HARRY: Remember we talked about leading earlier? How modern salespeople need to be able to lead customers? Well, I think as an account manager that kind of leadership is a key element and something that you want to want to bring into play.

LARRY: No arguments from here.

HARRY: Right. So next up, negotiation. I think it's an important skill for all salespeople, but certainly as an account manager. They could be negotiating on the regular basis, not just on terms and conditions, but probably more often these kind of problem-solving type negotiations. I might go as far as to say it's dealing with conflict, if you want to call it that. And of course, keeping focus. Results focus. Making sure we're delivering value, and that *we* are driving it. Driving it for the customer.

LARRY: That makes sense. Have you looked into customer success management? I have been reading a little bit about it recently.

HARRY: Hey, it's about time you taught me something.

LARRY: *[Laughs]* I am not an expert in it, but I know it's a growing discipline. It's about understanding what people are focused on, what are the outcomes of a project, what are we promising the customer and are we putting everything in place to make sure that happens? Because if we aren't, why are they going to want to come back to us? I know that some companies are setting up different roles, pure customer success managers, who are there to make sure the customer gets what we've promised.

HARRY: That is what we do though, isn't it?

LARRY: Well, it can be, though it depends on what the company structure is. What I'm reading about this, and the whole outcome focus it promotes, makes a lot of sense. Perhaps we as salespeople should understand this better.

HARRY: It sounds like I've got a bit of homework. I want to know more about this.

LARRY: Go for it.

HARRY: Well, for me, I'm doing it with my feedback calls, really understanding the customer and always delivering value. But I think there are probably other elements that we can bring into what we do to make sure we're delivering on an excellent level.

LARRY: Nice one. Well, it has been an interesting old time.

HARRY: It certainly has. And how are you feeling about it now?

LARRY: I'm feeling better than I did earlier in the year. I was very unhappy. I was very uncomfortable.

HARRY: I know that, Larry, and I didn't like seeing you like that.

LARRY: No, but you've been a help, you know. You've given me a bit of a roadmap.

HARRY: That's nice.

LARRY: You've been very generous in what you've shared. You've got your head around this stuff and then helped me with it.

HARRY: I don't know if I've got my head around it completely, but I'm becoming a lot clearer in how we need to work now.

LARRY: Yeah. I think I am too.

HARRY: So what are we saying? The way I see it is that we think of this as hybrid selling and we commit to getting good at it. We try to understand all these things that we can use. We get comfortable with all the elements that we potentially need to tap into to do the best possible things for our customers. That will reflect on ourselves and our own organisation. That for me, looks like the future. Hybrid selling seems to be where it is at.

LARRY: I think you're right. I don't think you can argue with that.

HARRY: Hybrid selling seems the way in which we need to go.

LARRY: Well, let's go get hybrid, then.

HARRY: Let's do it!

That was the last part of the ongoing conversation that helped Harry and Larry get their heads around something they started to call hybrid selling. Now they have put a name to it, their conversations are ongoing and they are far more positive. Harry keeps learning and keeps sharing. Larry now understands why he needs to implement subtle new ways of working and takes what Harry is sharing with a much more open mind. He is more receptive to new ideas and both are working together to develop themselves.

They know they are not the finished product. But they are looking towards the future, and they have a roadmap showing how they can evolve. They are essentially evolving by using the EVOLVE model:

- They understand the Essentials for success.

- They are applying Virtual selling skills, including video and social selling.

- They use Opportunity management techniques to keep track of what they are doing with customers so that they can add value.

- They are getting more and more comfortable in Leading customers; becoming servant leaders.

- They are helping the customers to really focus on Value.

- They are aware of the activity that will help them Expand and grow the business with their customers.

Harry and Larry are on the journey to develop their use of a hybrid selling approach. What about you?

PART 2
THE EVOLVE FRAMEWORK

Who are you going to be?

In this part of the book, I want to break down the EVOLVE framework to help you understand the key elements of an approach that will drive success in a modern selling environment.

A salesperson needs to embrace several different things, but no one said that selling is easy.

As professional selling becomes more involved and the skill set required more demanding, so the opportunity for the best to shine increases. Equally, the potential for failure is higher for those who are underprepared and underdeveloped to meet customer needs.

It is all about what type of salesperson you choose to be and how you grow into that role. This model will guide you.

7
Essentials For Success

When I was training salespeople at the turn of the century, I was in a privileged position as one of the courses I ran was the introduction that many would have had to the world of professional selling. It was the first training that many attended as they learned about the fundamentals.

They learned about understanding and selling benefits as a foundation before they should even start approaching customers. They learned about prospecting. They learned how to manage meetings. They learned about writing proposals and then how these can be presented with impact. They learned to plan and understand where business comes from, what the best opportunities are and how to qualify potential new business. They learned about self-management.

These essentials still ring true, and even though I was teaching them twenty years ago, fundamentally they are still the basis for good, solid selling. These are things in which we would expect salespeople to be competent today.

Now I would add that, because of the way that sales has evolved, collaborative selling is a prerequisite for success. People may say 'Of course you would, that's what you wrote your book *Selling through Partnering Skills* about'. But I wrote that book to show how professional salespeople can adopt the right mindset and develop an approach to be successful in selling today.

This chapter highlights those elements and guides people through the VALUE framework I now use to give people a solid basis for good professional selling.

Evolution of sales

Historically speaking

Sales, or at least some kind of trading or bartering, has been around since prehistoric times; a kind of 'swap my mammoth hide for your fishing basket' conversation. While this is interesting, it is not so useful to us when considering present-day sales, apart from the fact that even then transactions had to be based on needs or wants.

During the nineteenth century, the sales profession suffered a poor reputation. Between 1849 and 1882, some 180,000 Chinese immigrants travelled to America to help build the intercontinental railroad. With them they brought a product – snake oil. Clark Stanley, the original snake oil salesman, saw the opportunity to peddle this product and soon 'doctors' and travelling salesmen began to sell their magic remedies across the United States, using a number of unethical and questionable practices. Sadly, often salespeople still endure this stigma, even in today's more professional environment.

Let's look at the more recent developments in our quest to achieve success by applying things relevant to a hybrid selling approach. I will move to the middle of the twentieth century, when things got really interesting for professional salespeople.

Decades of progress

Sales techniques, and ways of working to ensure commercial success, have developed significantly since the Second World War. The timeline below gives an overview of how different ways of working have been employed by salespeople over the years.

1950s – process-focused (eg AIDA, attention, interest, desire, action)

1960s – personality-focused (use of psychology)

1970s – benefit-focused (motivation for buying)

1980s – closing-focused (objection handling)

1990s – needs-focused (consultative/solution selling)

2000s – value-focused (generating insight)

2010s – needs- and value-focused, plus proving 'sales stature' (including use of social media)

2020s – collaboration-focused (using partnering skills)

During the boom years of the 1950s, the focus was very much on having a solid methodology so that salespeople could repeat, time and again, the methods that worked. Arguably, this discipline started to develop in the 1920s when EK Strong published *The Psychology of Selling* and people began to take notice of a certain International Business Machines (IBM) and how they operated.[2] The idea that selling is a skill that could be learned, studied and mastered was further strengthened by the activities of Dale Carnegie (he of *How to Win Friends and Influence People*) in his role as a business trainer.[3]

The 1960s and its fascination with the mind saw the introduction of a more psychological approach to selling, with salespeople encouraged to use new skills to understand how a customer might be thinking and adapt their style to suit. Various models including DiSC, the Myers-Briggs Type Indicator (MBTI) and Social Styles were used to encourage salespeople to adopt the behavioural flex required to make their interactions more amenable to customers.

'What's in it for me?' was the customer's unspoken question that sales training during the 1970s urged salespeople to focus on. While not necessarily a new concept, this back-to-basics approach helped avoid the trap of speaking solely about the features a product or service might offer by translating these into benefits a customer would enjoy from the purchase. As advertising man Leo McGivena famously told his clients, 'People don't want to buy a quarter-inch drill. They want a quarter-inch hole.'[4]

One of the biggest innovations in the world of sales was the advent of 'consultative selling' techniques, which really came to the fore in the 1990s. This saw salespeople's activity shift towards the questioning and diagnostic skills required to uncover a customer's needs. It was a distinct move away from some of the approaches of the 1980s that had focused on the later parts of the sale, such as 'closing the deal' by 'handling objections'. Using questions in such a considered and structured way is known as both consultative and solution selling.

In the 2000s, those in a sales role were also encouraged to concentrate on how they could 'add value' for their customers. Using deeper 'contextual' or 'insightful' questions and considering the broader business benefits that can be delivered and designed into a wider solution are the principal means to achieve this.

For the 2010s, the consultative / adding value approach remained highly relevant, though anyone with a business development responsibility also needed to have an awareness of what was then referred to as 'Web 2.0' technology – particularly the use of social media. Newer means of communicating and sharing information played, and continue to play, an important part in how sales dialogue is undertaken. Customers are better informed, and salespeople are more likely to enter the process later in the buying cycle than ever before.

This evolution of sales into the 2020s sees an increasing shift towards a collaborative approach to working with customers. It involves creating more of a partnership between the salesperson and customer, one which makes sense for both parties over the longer term. By partnering with a salesperson and their organisation, the customer is likely to enjoy greater benefits by maintaining the business relationship and exploring more opportunities to create value. It means that a salesperson should be equipped with the right tools, techniques and (perhaps most important) mindset to achieve and maintain this partnership.

The VALUE framework

I have developed a framework that brings the skills required for the collaborative approach together with various methodologies and systems for selling that already exist. The synergy of the parts can give a salesperson a distinct advantage in how they go about winning business.

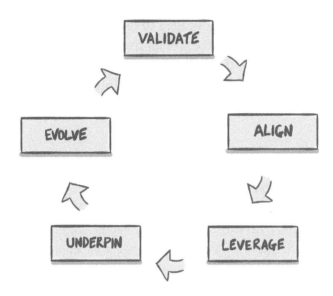

The VALUE framework is presented as a cycle rather than a phased progression, to show that selling often involves activity in parallel rather than in sequence. Sales tasks could well happen in order from Validating through to Evolving, and this may indeed be a way of programming activity in a simpler sale. However, many sales are more complex than that, with many things likely to be happening at once. This will be especially true when considering the type of business most salespeople will be aspiring to work on – repeat business. Delivering on one opportunity should involve setting up the next. In more complex sales it may also be necessary to 'jump forwards and backwards' to undertake activity necessary to keep the sale moving.

Salespeople are encouraged to use the VALUE framework to focus on the things that make a difference for customers and their own organisation. Doing this with a high degree of 'partnering intelligence' makes a better result for everyone.

Validate – How to check fit for doing business

Qualification

This part of the framework has its roots in sales 'qualification'. Essentially, does the customer or opportunity 'qualify' for my time and effort? Do they fulfil the necessary criteria that indicate the opportunity is both attractive and winnable? Is it going to be worth it?

In my experience, this is something that many salespeople find difficult to do. It is likely that the concept of 'qualifying out' an opportunity goes against the natural instincts of many who feel 'you have to be in it to win it'. But this is something that the best can do. Whether with a formal template or a finely tuned gut feeling, they know what makes good business and can decide on whether to progress or not. It is all about how to use that most precious of resources – time.

It takes two to tango

When we start to add the application of a more collaborative selling approach into the equation then Validation becomes even more important. Essentially, the salesperson is going to apply even more effort to winning the business by bringing this extra refinement to their approach and so needs to be sure that they get sufficient return on their investment. They will make the running with a selling style that requires a degree of reciprocity, and if it looks as though their efforts will not be returned then they ought to question whether it is worth trying to win the business.

This is not to say that all approaches should be disqualified, though it might well indicate that a more traditional or even transactional way of working is the best way ahead.

Psychological qualification

One way to look at this is that for each account or potential piece of business the salesperson should undertake a kind of psychological qualification. That is, assess how the business and those involved think and act during the buying and selling process and the period after a deal is done.

As well as looking at some of the more practical or quantitative criteria to help judge attractiveness/winnability I would advocate some more qualitative ones, to try to gauge thinking and operating style. Basically, are they going to be receptive to a sales approach strongly grounded in collaboration?

However, most of the success at this stage is down to the salesperson and their discipline. Even with all the information in the world pointing against it, an individual intent on pursuing an opportunity will do just that. They will justify investing their own and often their company's resources in chasing business that is, and always was, unlikely to be fruitful. For this reason the Validation stage is key in any form of professional sales.

Align – How we can work together

What's in it for me?

So, having decided that an opportunity looks valuable from all angles the next part of the framework encourages a salesperson to think about how they could potentially work with the customer. They need to establish what it is they might bring to the party. Fundamentals of sales tell us that if there is no benefit or if no need is being addressed then success is highly unlikely.

A good salesperson will do their research to try to understand the customer's business and start to work out what part of their wider offer they could talk about that will spark interest. It is here that mistakes are made by poor or inexperienced salespeople, who go in underprepared and hope a 'shotgun' approach – talking about everything – will do the job of interesting someone about something, sometime. It is amateur and a waste of time, and an approach that is not likely to be repeated with that customer any time soon as the door will remain firmly shut.

Equally, a self-centred approach will also fail. Over-reliance on knowledge of and/or fascination with their own company's offering will quickly become the downfall of a salesperson, however passionate they are about it. As the world gets faster and people get busier, customers want a speedy response to their (often unasked) question 'What's in it for me?' It is about being customer-centric and spending time thinking about them, for them, as them.

Delivering value

Research shows that as the complexity of the sale increases, so do the number of people involved in making the decision. The onus then falls on the salesperson to understand 'who's who' and what it is they are trying to achieve. A skilled sales practitioner will try to work out what levels of influence each customer contact has in terms both of power and of relative support.

In doing so a measure of how much value the deal may bestow on the customer begins to become clear and this becomes a key part of future interventions. Identifying and communicating value are integral parts of today's professional selling, and parts very much in harmony with the collaborative approach. It would be fair to say that high levels of market intelligence can be translated into high levels of partnering intelligence by a skilled operator.

Leverage – How to make a sales approach

Interaction to drive action

At some stage, desk work must be translated into leg work, preparation into action. The customer, if not already involved in some elements of the research, must now take position at the front and centre of sales activity.

With a high degree of preparation undertaken and high levels of insight generated a salesperson may feel they know a customer's business well. They might be right. They might be tempted to prepare an elegant pitch to showcase this knowledge. This would be the wrong thing to do.

Now, I am not saying that this knowledge should not be used; success is about how it is used. A skilled practitioner will use this insight to demonstrate competence and heighten their credibility. But above all they will use it to engage and involve the customer. A multitude of maxims and models extol the virtues of 'listen before talk', 'be in discovery mode' or 'uncover the need', and they are right. This is absolutely the right approach and one completely in line with a collaborative way of working.

It's good to talk

Or so we were told by a large advertising campaign for UK telecommunications giant BT in the 1990s. We also know that talking is the cornerstone of great relationships. The Leverage part of the framework encourages exactly that. Better communication breeds better understanding and understanding in turn breeds better relationships. Building better relationships is a key part of collaboration, so this element of the VALUE framework is essential.

Understanding the customer is important in any sale. This can be at a shallow level – 'know problem; fix problem' – to the far deeper knowledge of what makes them tick and being able to respond on this level as well as on the practical level. Every sales methodology worth its salt encourages some kind of engagement with the relevant people. In today's environment a salesperson, like a good boy scout, has 'to be prepared', as customers will not want to waste time giving information that is readily available. Core to success is the ability to interact with other human beings.

Underpin – How to present, prove and agree

Underpin: verb

1. Support (a building or other structure) from below by laying a solid foundation below ground level or by substituting stronger for weaker materials.

2. Support, justify or form the basis for.[5]

In the VALUE framework I am talking about the second definition (though I also like the concept of substituting stronger for weaker materials when considering a competitive selling environment).

Getting the message across

This is all about being able to show and substantiate reasons to do business together, which should be presented in a way that is attractive to the customer. It is here that the wheels come off for many salespeople.

Even those with great engagement and discovery skills, those that generate insight and use it to develop mutual value, can mess up a presentation. This can often be down to self-centred behaviour: something like 'We do this, we do that, we do the other', all about the salesperson and their own organisation. At this stage, you must be customer-centric. A good salesperson should talk about the customer, the customer's interests, the customer's issues and THEN align with what they can do to help address these.

Making it easy to say yes

Top salespeople make it easy to say yes by making it all about the customer.

If a customer can understand and see value, it is easier for them to say yes. If it is clear how it is proposed to work together and this looks hassle-free, it is easier to say yes. If a seller's proposition is different to others that the customer may receive it is then easier for them to say yes. (If it is truly unique this is even better!) Essentially, if what a salesperson says is believable, if it is proven, if it carries little risk, it is easier to say yes.

Evolve – How to develop the business

Long-term focus

The VALUE framework carries an implicit long-term focus. It is not about quick one-sided wins – though there is nothing wrong with increasing speed to mutual benefit.

Proposed business and means of working together should include regular and scheduled reviews. By reviews we mean a thorough diagnosis of how business together is going and what can be done to improve things. This is not a quick scan over half a dozen service-level agreements (SLAs) and a self-congratulatory 'didn't we do well?' This is about a proper, deep dive into activities and relationships. It is something that should be taken seriously with dates set in stone and attendance expected from senior personnel from both parties. This both indicates how important the reviews are and will allow problems to be rectified and opportunities to be capitalised upon – fast.

Having structure to the discussions and pertinent measurements to guide will facilitate this process, one that should be approached with the appropriate mindset, of genuinely wanting to work together towards a common goal, not an 'us and them' mentality. The purpose of these interventions is to strengthen ties and seek opportunities to get more from the relationship. I once described this, and the comment was 'Oh, like a corporate date night'. It made me smile and though I do sometimes use that terminology there is another I use more often – a partnering approach.

Celebrating success

What do these have in common? Paper, cotton, leather, fruit, wood, sugar, wool, metal, pottery, aluminium. In the UK they are all symbols of wedding anniversaries (first to tenth).

So how do we celebrate success and longevity in business relationships? That is a tough one to answer as there is no formal or codified system like that for marriage. While I am not necessarily advocating anything as symbolic, I am certainly all for recognising and celebrating successes in business and companies working together. In doing this the relationships can be strengthened and built upon for future success.

The key to this is doing it *together*, not the sales organisation patting itself on the back and counting the revenue earned. This is about both parties looking at the value that has been generated, how this has occurred and planning to make it happen again and again.

Addressing failure

So, everything in the garden is rosy, all the time. Happy days are here again.

It would be naïve to assume that any approach could guarantee this. In any relationship there may be tough times. It is how these are addressed that counts. Intercepting issues early and dealing with them proactively is the way to make the most of relationships and a trait of those who understand collaboration. This does not involve ignoring things and hoping the problem goes away, as it rarely will. It is about addressing and dealing with them.

Yet again a structured and deliberate approach to checking how we are working together and making the most of it will be the key to (customer) success.

Why the VALUE framework delivers

The VALUE framework works. It works because of its component parts. Indeed, it is more than the sum of its parts and this synergy gives a salesperson an up-to-date approach to successful selling.

As complexity and value increase, so the type of sales changes and recommended best practice alters. Hours and hours of research have gone into understanding the most effective way for a sales professional to operate and the VALUE framework is designed to capture these, bring them into play and encourage them to be applied with a high degree of customer-centricity. The use of partnering skills alongside other sales skills gives extra finesse, the salesperson brings something extra to the table and that something extra can make the difference between winning or losing business.

Using partnering skills

Making the journey smoother

Most of us don't spend a lot of time analysing our relationships, business or otherwise. They just happen. They form and evolve and, before we know it, they fall into familiar patterns. By being more conscious about the nature of relationships we can make deliberate adjustments to what we say and do, to make the journey smoother.

Partnering Intelligence

The concept of Partnering Intelligence can be attributed to work by Steve Dent in the 1990s and is outlined in his book *Partnering Intelligence: Creating value for your business by building smart alliances.*[6] It is based on six elements that make up a behaviour-based system that results in an environment conducive to building trust and creating mutual beneficial relationships. It is important to be 'fluent and fluid' in all six elements in order to reap the benefits, since the six elements build on and reinforce each other. They are:

- Trust

- Win–win orientation

- Comfort with interdependence

- Self-disclosure and feedback

- Comfort with change

- Future orientation

The six elements of effective partnering

Let's look at these six elements in more detail.

They are based on four years of research conducted from 1988 to 1992 with more than 2,000 middle and upper-level executives and elected union officials from different geographic and cultural areas who needed to partner with each other. This research was expanded to include other executives, nonprofit and community leaders from 1992 to 1998.

Trust

As trust is the basis for all healthy and productive relationships it is also the key to enabling yourself and others to use the six partnering elements effectively.

Without trust, you cannot achieve real collaboration. Trust must be both put into the relationship and result from it.

Win-win orientation

This means building trust and finding an outcome that is a win for both the salesperson and their customer. To do this we must overcome both inherited and conditioned reactions to disagreements as though they were threats. Instead of 'fight or flight', we can develop responses to reason, needs and communication that overcome our instincts and emotional stress. If we do not, we create losers, not winners.

Comfort with interdependence

This is all about collaboration, striking a balance between teamwork and individual input. This element helps us learn how to be independent (play our individual part) and dependent too (trust and rely on partners, both in our own organisation and in customers). When we get this right, the whole can be greater than the sum of the parts.

Self-disclosure and feedback

I have stressed communication several times, and how we communicate is as crucial as what we try to communicate. This includes honestly sharing relevant, personal and business information, providing honest feedback at appropriate times and in appropriate ways and listening to feedback we receive. This will help build trust.

Comfort with change

This is the flip side to comfort with interdependence. Change is always with us. You need to understand how you respond to change (is your instinct to start it? adapt to it? or resist it?) and be prepared: you may need strategies to tone down or compensate for your instincts. Your customer may see these instincts in you, and respect or despise how you control them (or fail to).

Future orientation

Salespeople and organisations that get stuck in the past become demoralised and left behind. It is good to look to the future, but crucial for you and your customer to hold each other accountable for results, in order to trust and learn to collaborate with each other.

A sales ethos

Ethos is a Greek word meaning 'character'. It is used to describe the guiding beliefs or ideals that characterise a community, nation or ideology. In modern usage, ethos indicates the disposition or fundamental values peculiar to a specific person, people, organisation or movement.

A salesperson can use partnering skills to define their ethos, their approach to selling. Understanding partnering skills can help to make that definition and develop it in a way conducive to winning business in today's commercial world.

Isn't this something that is already trained? Something that is implicit in the way salespeople operate?

Well, the answer is 'yes', or at least it should be. The point is that selling can be more effective if it becomes explicit. Salespeople can benefit from a deliberate, conscious approach using partnering skills as their foundation to whatever type of sale they are engaged in.

Summary

Good selling comes from having a solid basis. It is all about having the essentials for success.

A sales professional can develop these by

- Understanding past trends in selling and what is useful today

- Using the VALUE framework as a means of codifying and developing their approach:
    - Validate – check fitness for doing business
    - Align – preparing to work together
    - Leverage – making a sales approach
    - Underpin – present, prove and agree
    - Evolve – develop the business

- Developing partnering skills to drive ethos and behaviours in today's sales environment.

Are you working from a strong foundation as an up-to-date sales professional?

8
Virtual Selling

Virtual selling is now part and parcel of the way that we operate. This term is now widely used in several ways, so the definition I use in this book is about how we can operate using the tools and the techniques given to us by modern technology. The phone is included in this, as is email and now of course video conferencing.

It requires skill in leveraging the technology now available. I would say that a professional salesperson needs more than just competence in delivering messages, having conversations and inspiring collaboration using different media. To be successful you must move from OK to good to excellent.

An area that is getting more attention and that sales-people who are embracing it are finding extremely effective is the use of video. Recording and sending messages can deliver a number of benefits and we will look at how and why.

I am also going to cover 'social selling' in this section. This is using technology and the social media platforms available to build and to influence relationships. I think primarily, for most B2B salespeople, this means LinkedIn (though in some sectors Facebook, Instagram and Twitter might be relevant; YouTube can also be an important platform). Again, the aspiration should be more than just competence.

Other technology including artificial intelligence (AI) is also available to the modern salesperson to help them focus and save time on what they do. Though much is beyond the scope of this book and the speed of development extremely fast we will consider some things to take advantage of.

Online meetings

The big five

'What are the 'big five' you would want to see on an African safari?'

I often ask this question on training sessions, to encourage participants to put responses in the Chat.

(Encouraging the use of Chat in larger presentations is a great way to keep people involved and get instant feedback.) It never ceases to amuse when 'tiger' is among the answers, but the reason I ask is to set up a discussion around key elements to consider when involved in a virtual meeting. While we might want to see a lion, leopard, rhinoceros, elephant and buffalo on our safari, for meetings the big five are

- Video

- Audio

- Lighting

- Background

- Self

Video should be on whenever possible, and participants encouraged to turn the video on at their end. Not only is it easier to read people but research has shown that people are more engaged when on camera as psychologically they feel more 'in the meeting'.[7] Setting expectations in advance helps. Ideally, you should use a high-definition (HD) webcam, set at eye level with your head centred. Looking into the lens is the equivalent of eye contact, so it is worth considering when to do that. When the camera on it is best to leave it on and stay in the picture, remembering you are on show to all participants. Try to avoid looking at yourself and concentrate on the matter in hand.

Audio is as important as video, if not more so. If people cannot hear they soon lose interest, as it is tiring to strain to hear and when people cannot hear someone properly, they perceive the speaker as less credible. Not what we want as professional salespeople. Therefore, a good microphone is important, either an external mic or one mounted in a headset, and noise-cancelling varieties are good. Many people prefer to use 'ear buds', which will usually be better than the internal speaker built into the computer. Try to minimise background noise and turn off notifications. Using mute when not speaking is an option, but stay alert: 'you are on mute' was probably the most used phrase in 2020!

Use fixed **lighting** so other participants can see you. The whole point is better communication, so make sure that you can use the important nonverbal communication that comes from the face. A ring light is reasonably cheap and easy to position to give extra brightness with balance. Be aware of overhead and back-lighting as having a conversation with a silhouette akin to a Bond villain is not ideal for a meeting and shows poor preparation and understanding of the medium.

Backgrounds can say a lot about a person. Ever had a call with a person 'sat in space' or 'on the beach'? Exactly. Virtual backgrounds can be effective and well-thought-out backgrounds that use logos (or something that indicates consideration of the customer) can work.

However, most people now seem to prefer talking to people in their natural environment (we are curious creatures), so as long as that is tidy natural seems to be the preferred option. 'Working from home' or indeed 'from anywhere' is now increasingly accepted.

You are key to a successful meeting. The other elements can be set up once, and go on giving the proper impression, but this element deserves attention every time. Clothing should be chosen to appear professional and neither blend into the background nor look fuzzy on camera. Distance from the camera and posture are also considerations, with enough space to not appear too big or small and to allow effective use of gestures. Controlled use of hand gestures is encouraged just as it would be if we were in the same room: it aids communication, so be sure not to lose body language cues that help others understand more effectively. Good posture helps with this as well as looking and staying alert. Standing up, facing raised cameras with screens behind, is becoming increasingly popular as it brings energy and has health benefits. Above all, stay present. It is easy to get distracted and people will notice.

Leading collaboration

Knowing how to stimulate collaboration and creativity at online meetings can take effectiveness to another level. It will improve the customer's perception of a salesperson's general competence if they can manage this space well.

While tools such as Microsoft Whiteboard, Miro and Murali are excellent, even taking notes 'on screen' into a Word document or PowerPoint slide has a positive effect as the customer feels part of the conversation and takes greater ownership of the outcome. These tools take a little practice and confidence, but it does not have to be perfect as it shows authenticity. Leading collaboration is something that can really set a meeting apart.

Video messaging

The perfect storm

Using recorded video is another great option for salespeople. When it comes to video and a thoroughly modern approach to selling Mario Martinez Jr, the CEO of Vengreso and a modern sales evangelist, is one of my go-to guys. When I interviewed him, he explained to me how a number of things have happened to make the use of video so important; now, we are:

- Digitally connected – most people have more than one device connected to the internet

- Socially engaged – many people also have one or more social media platforms

- Mobile attached – time spent using a mobile phone is at an all-time high (and not for just talking)

- Video-hungry – people like watching video.

If a salesperson is not incorporating video into their way of working, they are missing a trick. The tools are at their fingertips, yet many seem reluctant to use them.

The visual sale

Perhaps part of the reluctance to do this is not really knowing how to. Essentially the technique is to look at a camera and speak. So, in a quest to understand more and be able to pass on best practice I spoke to Tyler Lessard who, with Marcus Sheridan, wrote *The Visual Sale*.[8] This book is a great resource that covers both sales and marketing. Tyler explained that good videos for both disciplines share some common characteristics; they are

- Engaging – our brains are hard-wired for stories so a good video should have an element of storytelling; introducing a problem or issue and showing how to deal with it is a simple version of a story.

- Emotional – 'emotion drives motion' so think about how you want a viewer to feel after watching your video: this is an opportunity to make a deeper connection with customers.

- Educational – we are more geared to process visual information than text, so a video is usually more fun and efficient than working through a written document; images are processed straight into long-term memory rather than short-term, where text is dealt with.

- Empathetic – great content shows that you understand the viewer; a great salesperson should understand the customer and their challenges, and video lets you show that understanding.

Tyler refers to these as the 'superpowers of video' and recommends trying to hit two or three with every video created as a means of driving the action you want. All the better if you can incorporate all four!

Synchronous and asynchronous communication

These terms are used to describe how a salesperson can be 'in front' of their customer on video. It brings a new dynamic to how salespeople must think about communicating.

Synchronous communications are two-way communications in which participants can converse with each other in real time. This might be a Zoom or Teams call. The advantage of synchronous/real-time communication is interactivity and the ability to get feedback and collaborate instantly.

Asynchronous communications are back-and-forth exchanges with a delay between messages, or one-way communications that can be received by an audience at their convenience, such as live streams and webinars that are delivered one-to-many, or a specific video recording. Video on demand, like email and other text documents, can be viewed at any time, from any location, and it can be searched and watched again later. It is a way of providing rich and detailed information with a human touch.

And most importantly, it can be shared. This last fact is not lost on salespeople, who use video as an effective means to get their message heard by the increasing number of stakeholders now involved in a typical sale.

Video can be used to 'power up' many aspects of the sales process such as engaging and connecting with prospects, setting an agenda for meetings, to recap a meeting, delivering a proposal, sharing success stories, thanking and recognising your best customers. In fact, if you could say it live, you can create a video.

Just do it

This famous slogan seems apt in encouraging salespeople to adopt this powerful technique. To inspire some quick wins, I have combined some of the tips Mario and Tyler shared with me with some other ideas I have come across, which I hope will help you make the most of this exciting way to add a new dimension to your selling and help you stand out.

1. **Get the 'production' basics right** – At the most basic, you need to make sure you're seen, heard and taken seriously in your sales videos.

2. **Capture attention with thumbnails** – Be creative. Think what will make someone want to watch.

3. **Be interesting!** – Once they have started watching the viewer needs to be engaged. Get to the point fast, tell them what they're going to get from the video or ask relevant questions.

4. **Tailor your video and message to the audience** – Same as it ever was. If you are going to talk about your product or service, do so in the context of their challenges.

5. **Answer frequently asked questions** – Many customer questions are going to be the same, time and again. Having videos ready to answer these saves time and is a useful resource.

6. **Add personality to emails** – What better way to put yourself in front of people and show you care than sending a personalised video? (Don't tell them it is often easier than writing something, as well as more effective.)

7. **Make science work for you** – 'Mirror neurons' cause us to do something when we observe someone else doing it, like smiling or laughing. If someone smiles at you, they prompt you to smile back. The brain does not differentiate between

something that you observe on a screen and something that happens in person.

Social selling and personal branding

What is social selling?

Ask 100 social media experts and you will probably get 100 different answers. A few of these are:

'Think of social selling as modern relationship-building. Actively connecting with potential customers on social media can help you be the first brand a prospect considers when they're ready to make a purchase.'
— Christina Newberry and Karin Olafson[9]

'Selling on social media platforms is not unlike any other form of selling… Being genuine, showing real interest, and understanding the psychology behind what people need to be willing to engage with you is the secret sauce.'
— Alexander Low, Death of a Salesman podcast[10]

'Social selling is not a replacement for any single sales activity. It is a tool that can be utilised at different parts of the sales process to compliment, enhance or modernise it.'
— Daniel Disney, *The Ultimate LinkedIn Sales Guide*[11]

I like these as they talk about using the tools and techniques in addition to all the other elements of professional selling, rather than as a 'be all and end all', which can be suggested by more naïve operators or self-proclaimed 'gurus' who do not really understand selling.

Daniel lays the key elements out in five key areas:

1. **Personal brand** – To say who you are and show that you are credible.

2. **Network** – The people that read or listen to what you say.

3. **Content** – Both curated (someone else created it; you share it) and created by you. You build and engage your network through providing content.

4. **Conversation** – Crucial: how you turn contacts into prospects and work through the sales cycle.

5. **Research** – Find out about contacts using social media; qualify prospects and keep up with customers.

I capture this in the PEN WOP FOP model for salespeople.

PEN WOP FOP model

Years ago, I worked in the beer trade running the 'Coronacademy'. To help salespeople sell beer into the 'off-trade' (supermarkets and multiples) we used a model focusing on market penetration (PEN), encouraging people to buy more (WOP or weight of purchase) and to buy more often (FOP or frequency of purchase).

I have modified it for B2B salespeople using social media to assist selling:

PEN: Platform – choose the right place to be and create the right profile

WOP: Weight of Posting – how valuable or useful to people your content is

FOP: Frequency of Posting – how often you add content.

Each of these can be taken to great depth and unsurprisingly platforms offer a lot of information about how to use the platform (though choose advice wisely).

There is a very high-level guide using LinkedIn as the platform of choice, as many B2B salespeople and their customers already use it.

PEN/Platform

Your LinkedIn profile is effectively your landing page; everyone who clicks your name or picture in their feed will be taken to it.

Just like a website landing page it should clearly show what you do, the problems you solve, how you make customers' lives better; and make it easy for visitors to contact you. Key for your LinkedIn profile are:

- **Profile banner** – this is an important bit of 'real estate', showing how you help people and businesses, and your contact info

- **Profile photo** – use a professional, clear headshot, not a selfie or holiday snap; this is seen by everyone in the feed and when they take the time to click your profile

- **Headline** – a hook for your content and comments on other people's content that should let people quickly understand what you do and whether you are interesting to them

- **Providing services section** – pick key services that are relevant to what you offer

- **About** – think landing page; make it customer-centric; an effective structure is:

  - Start with your ideal customers' frustrations

  - How you help; your services

  - Social proof / case study

  - How to get in touch

- **Featured** – your chance to sell: add your website link, email sign-up, useful videos, any links that can help people do business with you, learn more about you or start a conversation with you

- **Recommendations** – ask customers to leave reviews to help build trust in people checking your profile (try encouraging them to explain the problems they had before working with you, why they decided to work with you and what their business/life is now like after working with you).

WOP/Weight of Posting

You can create your own content or like/share/comment on other people's. An intelligent comment on a good post can be valuable, but creating your own content will have greater impact. There are around 760 million members on LinkedIn, yet only around 1% of them share content regularly; so just by posting on a regular basis you put yourself in the top 1%.

Content can take the form of:

- Text only
- Images
- Video
- PDF/slides
- Polls
- Articles

When creating content think about what you are trying to achieve and whether it will:

- Ease – help people with something
- Educate – teach people something
- Entertain – just amuse them for a moment

There is nothing wrong with producing content to entertain people. It shows a human and personal side. It is called 'social' media for a reason. However, as a sales professional, try to strike a balance between being useful and being fun.

Some people find it difficult to start writing. Use these as thought starters:

- Problems that customers have
- Real questions customers ask
- Real conversations with customers
- Testimonials
- Case studies
- Past mistakes
- Useful tips (how to do X, 5 ways to do Y, how to avoid Z)
- Useful strategies
- Best practice

Essentially, anything you might say to one person in a meeting can be shared with many at once and boost the perception people have of who you are and what you do.

FOP/Frequency of Posting

Aim to post once a day.

Set some time aside and use this to create a post and comment on others. Also, use this time to search for and connect with interesting people (because they are potential customers and/or share useful material you can learn from).

Remember this is an investment of time and play the long game. Despite what some coaches and trainers might imply people probably won't come flocking to your door. However, by making this little extra effort you are continually building your profile, network and potential to influence people.

AI and other assistance

Have you ever wondered how AI impacts the world of sales?

As you probably already know, AI is one of the key tech trends right now. It is already implemented and used in different business processes such as industrial automation, healthcare and other areas, but this technology can also help us out in sales, which is a really exciting opportunity.

The world of selling is going to look very different in the future. That's not an unfounded claim – it's based on the fact that AI and machine learning are fast reaching a level of sophistication which will make traditional selling methods obsolete.

AI and machine learning are emerging and will ultimately revolutionise the way we do business. The growth of this technology isn't limited to large corporations, either. These tools are already being leveraged by small businesses, startups and even individuals to scale their business.

AI has been around for decades, but it wasn't until recently that it reached our smartphones in the form of virtual assistants. These assistants are designed to help us check the weather, schedule meetings and even chat to us about movies. From there, giving sales teams access to AI became almost inevitable.

Fair disclosure – this is the first part of this section that I am writing myself. Everything preceding this was done by a machine. All I did was cut and paste.

I used a product called Copy.ai and having chosen what output I wanted (a blog introduction) I primed it by describing what I wanted (*'AI in selling. How artificial intelligence impacts the world of sales'*) and it did the rest, providing these snippets and others in under 30 seconds. The point of sharing this is to show how AI can do the heavy lifting for us.

However, I appreciate that this frightens and confuses many people. Perhaps through lack of understanding, perhaps through feeling threatened that the machines will take over. But AI is already a part of our lives, through managing what we see on social media feeds, recommending music/films/TV, controlling lights and security settings at home, helping make travel bookings and many more areas.

It is way beyond the scope of this book to look at exactly how AI can help in sales, and it would quickly date the publication as the rate of change and development is phenomenal. Applications include:

Prediction/forecasting

Systems exist that can predict or forecast outcomes using historical data to inform future results. Common predictions that sales AI systems can make include:

- Opportunities or prospects most likely to close

- Opportunities or prospects to target next

- New customers that may be interested

Lead scoring and prioritisation

Machines can look dispassionately at large quantities of data from different sources and inform salespeople what opportunities to prioritise. This helps avoid the waste of resources when decisions are made emotionally and with incomplete information.

Making recommendations

As well as predicting and prioritising, some AI systems may recommend which sales actions make most sense, based on goals and insights from the data. These recommendations could include:

- Advice on how to price an opportunity

- Who to target next

- Which customers to target with up-sells or cross-sells

Performance and productivity enhancement

AI can automate or augment work and allow salespeople to concentrate on higher-value tasks. This can include managing diaries, assessing sales pipelines or generating communications. It can also be used to analyse calls and meetings, to capture insight and help salespeople develop faster.

The potential is huge and can be daunting, but we should embrace it in selling just as we do in other areas.

Let it do the hard work and use the time saved to concentrate on the things that are uniquely human: like putting information into context, generating different perspectives and building relationships. Use AI to augment the human.

Summary

Technology is here to help us.

A modern salesperson will make the effort to understand and use the wide variety of technological opportunities available to them. In doing so they can appear progressive and appealing to customers, up to date and current. By not doing so they can come across as old-fashioned and create a negative impression on customers. Things to consider include:

- Becoming excellent at running online meetings using video conference technology

- Recording, sending and posting videos

- Making the most of opportunities social media offers to improve communication and customer contact

- Using tools to help with some of the tasks machines can do better and faster than we can

Are you using everything available to augment yourself as a sales professional?

9

Opportunity Management

Opportunity management is different to account management. There are plenty of similarities, but opportunity management focuses on a particular opportunity or specific project. It is about progressing an identified chance to win business. To help focus on this more effectively I use what I call the 'nine-box model' to encourage salespeople to think about the opportunity they have in greater depth and decide on the actions required to win the business.

We need to manage information and recognise what we know and what we don't. The thinking can be driven through a number of levels which helps the salesperson make sense of the opportunity. Information is considered around data, DMU and decisions.

This ability to use information to take opportunities and manage them through to a successful outcome is a key area of modern selling. Having a structure for this helps.

Information and 'known unknowns'

Knowledge is power

Good selling is all about information: providing information that is relevant and useful to customers and understanding what we know and what we don't know. If we recognise that we have things we need to understand better, this becomes a challenge – a challenge to find out. It should direct where we go and what we do to try to learn more.

The gap may relate to a competitor. It may be the way a company operates, their targets, vision, goals etc. More than likely, it is going to be around the DMU.

Understanding the people involved in making the decision is key. How do they do that? What are they thinking? What's important to them? What challenges do they have? What issues or concerns exist? What goals? What aspirations? As a salesperson, the more we understand this, the better a job we can do. We can work out how they make decisions. We can help them make decisions. And this in turn affects our own decisions. It guides the actions that we are going to take to move the opportunity forward.

Known unknowns

At a news briefing in 2002, United States Secretary of Defense Donald Rumsfeld said:

> '...there are known knowns; there are things we know we know. We also know there are known unknowns; that is to say we know there are some things we do not know. But there are also unknown unknowns – the ones we don't know we don't know.'[12]

He was talking about national security but could easily have been describing a typical sales opportunity.

This is the value that a good salesperson brings to the party – making sense of things. From a selling perspective these would be:

1. **Known knowns** – having a good plan and disciplined use of customer relationship management (CRM).

2. **Known unknowns** – things we have been trying to find out, but the customer will not tell us – perhaps it is early in the relationship, perhaps it suits them not to; and external factors that need considering.

3. **Unknown knowns** – if only we knew what we know! Sometimes an organisation might have valuable information but not realise it; knowledge could be held by different individuals or

departments that, when pieced together, could make the next steps in an opportunity far easier to define.

4. **Unknown unknowns** – might help us or might harm us. We know they are there but their nature makes them hard to define, so reducing them through capturing market intelligence and sharing what we do know puts us in a better position to operate effectively for everyone's benefit.

Nine-box model

The model is a means to think about capturing information and focusing activity.

Data	Opportunity	Competition	Position
DMU	People	Needs	Influence
Decisions	Summary	Possible	Best

It is a live document designed to hold and share information, structure thinking and drive meaningful actions. Working through and revisiting each of the boxes allows a salesperson and their team to consider how to progress.

Data – Opportunity

Information in this section is about qualifying the potential and defining the 'single sales objective', the aim for that particular opportunity, including the expected revenue figure and the expected close date. Any well-formed objective should be

SMART (specific, measurable, achievable, relevant, timebound).

While it is not the same as the overall account objective the single sales objective would contribute towards achieving that and broader business goals.

Data – Competition

Who and what (bearing in mind that other ways of achieving goals and 'do nothing' are options for the customer).

This thinking becomes more effective when 'positives' and 'negatives' are considered from the point of view of the customer.

Data – Position

'Where are we now?' in likelihood of winning the business. This can be captured on a scale such as:

Great > Secure > Comfortable > OK > Uncomfortable > Worried

Other analyses such as SWOT, Trend or RESPECT can be used to inform this.

DMU – People

Everyone who has any influence on the decision.

More people are usually involved than most sales-people think.

DMU - Needs

Explore this in detail, to try to satisfy individuals on every level. Consider needs, wants, issues, concerns, challenges, hopes, fears, ambitions.

This captures logical and emotional drivers at business and personal levels.

DMU - Influence

Like or dislike? Help or hinder?

Work out the whether the individual is supportive or not and consider the strength of the influence they have.

Decisions - Summary

What information is missing? What have we learned already?

This is a chance to consider what the analysis of the opportunity has already brought to light.

Decisions - Possible

What actions are required?

Share information with colleagues and brainstorm what to do next. Think about activities that might need to take place internally as well with the customer.

Decisions – Best

The basis of the plan.

Defining who needs to know or do what and how, to take control of sharing this information and driving activity in a timely and relevant manner.

Remember, the nine-box model is a live model. It should constantly evolve as more information is added, to capture the constant change experienced in any opportunity. It is a classic example of 'you get out what you put in'.

As the people/DMU element is so important we will give this a section to itself.

Decision-making units

What is a DMU?

Traditionally salespeople concentrated on a 'decision maker'. However, research is showing that increasingly more people are involved, so we need to consider DMUs.[13]

Within a DMU an individual may have a stronger *influence*, but everyone should be considered important, and their individual objectives, needs, wants, key performance indicators (KPIs) – whatever it is they are trying to achieve – should be understood. By doing this a salesperson can start to think more strategically about their approach by understanding who might be a:

- **Supporter**: someone who likes what the salesperson is offering and will push for that decision

- **Detractor**: the opposite of a supporter, who will do what they can to make what the salesperson is offering not happen

- **Influencer**: neutral in allegiance, but having things they want to achieve, and their opinion counts

- **Sponsor/coach**: like a 'super supporter' who will work hard to help and even on behalf of the salesperson

So how does the salesperson work out who is who? They map the DMU.

Mapping a DMU

One effective way to do this is to draw an organigram and try to assign bits of information to each individual that could have an influence. Lots of different pieces of information could be captured and potentially all would be useful. The following are what a salesperson should aspire to understand as a minimum.

1. **Name**: Everybody has one, it is how we are identified. It is important when dealing with people that we use it and get it right.

2. **Title**: Different companies label different jobs with different titles. We want to work in a way consistent with their approach and demonstrate we are willing to do so. Whatever the title, we should also get a clue as to the function the person actually performs. For some people it is almost as important to get their title right as to get their name right.

3. **Role**: People will play a different role *in how the decision is made*. This is not the same as their job, which we capture in 'Title'. It is related to the influence they have with the DMU. Specific labels help focus on this:

    -   'Users' tend to be people who have hands-on experience with the product or service.

    -   'Criteria buyers' have different 'criteria' that need fulfilling, perhaps 'commercial' – buy at X price, make Y margin, pay in Z days – or 'technical' – specification, functionality, packaging required.

- 'Economic buyers', the people that bring all the various opinions together to ultimately make the decision.

- 'Coach' can be one of the other roles or someone different who really helps the sale, giving extra information, lending support, opening doors and the like.

Economic buyers have the final say so there tends to only be one. We deliberately avoid the use of 'decision maker' as the whole point is to understand the 'unit' and its dynamics rather than focusing on one individual who may seem to have all the control but is really relying on the input of others.

1. **Influence**: This can be graded on a scale of 1–10: for = 10, against = 1. It can also be useful to gauge how *strong* that influence is (again on a scale of 1–10), so indicating whether that person is a detractor or a supporter.

2. **Personality**: It is useful to recognise personal style as it means the salesperson can quickly adjust behaviours to fit with individuals.

3. **WIIFM**: 'What's in it for me?' Answering this question for all concerned is a key to successful selling. Can also be expressed as their particular *Win*.

Finding out this information tells the salesperson who they need to know more about and how to tailor their approach.

It can also be quite a frightening experience when some realise that they are not as close to their customers as they think. The expletives uttered on many a training course when participants do this for the first time are testament to this!

Using mutual action plans

Perhaps one of the most underused tools by salespeople is the mutual action plan. These are extremely powerful ways to position value and drive the activity to deliver it. As a living document, the plan defines key activities associated with each milestone that will allow a customer to make an informed purchasing decision and achieve their desired outcomes.

They work well as buying is not easy, and becoming increasingly complicated. Often a customer will not know all the elements involved – the decision criteria to be considered, the internal process, activities to allow for effective implementation and how to get various interested parties working together. Anything to help make a better decision while reducing internal friction and risk will be welcomed.

Tom Williams, author of *The Seller's Challenge* and *Buying-Centred Selling*,[14] is a big fan of mutual action plans or, as he likes to call them, 'outcome engagement plans'. (They also go by the names mutual success plan, collaboration, close plan, customer journey plan, go live plan, deal plan and project plan.) Having sat on both sides of the table he is a strong advocate, as he knows they help the customer make an informed, step-by-step decision by providing insight and direction while firmly placing the salesperson in control of the sales process. In an interview he outlined the components he likes to see included:

1. Plan owners

2. Situation and value

3. Stakeholders

4. Commitments (required and agreed to)

5. Barriers to change

6. Major milestones (activities, time frames and results)

7. Deliverables

Let's break these down:

Plan owners should record the name and titles of the main contact and the salesperson. Ideally the contact is a champion for change within their organisation and has influence.

Situation and value is derived from good selling. The salesperson works with the customer to understand:

- *Current state*: what is the problem, opportunity or threat (POT)?

- *Root cause*: why is this happening?

- *Desired future state*: what is the desired outcome and the value desired?

- *Impact*: what happens if a change doesn't occur: business implications, eg impact on revenue, cost or risk?

- *Owner of the POT*: record names, titles and department.

- *Priority and urgency*: is this an individual, department, or company priority; irritating, important or critical?

Stakeholders make up the DMU. The salesperson recognises how they are impacted by the opportunity.

Commitments required and agreed to captures the resources and communication required. When these are agreed to up front sales opportunities move more quickly and 'no decision' is less likely. These may include:

- *Time*: agree to invest the time to work together

- *Change*: agree that a change is required and is an organisational priority

- *Collaboration*: commit to co-creating potential solutions and resolving concerns

- *Identify stakeholders*: everyone impacted by the opportunity

- *Access*: facilitate introductions and access to all stakeholders identified

- *Build consensus*: agree to work together to build consensus around the need for change, the requirements to be met and the preferred solution

- *Investment*: agree that the organisation will invest in a solution

- *Identify barriers to change*: these may be risks and concerns; work together to mitigate them

- *Decision criteria*: identify the evaluation process and decision criteria in detail

- *Decision process*: agree the decision process for a purchase if all the decision criteria are met

Major milestones will vary as each plan is different in levels of complexity. This tracker should also identify and include any deliverables that must be provided by either party. The last milestone should be the 'outcome desired' and NOT 'contract signed'. The milestones and activities should include all demos and presentations, procurement requirements, execution or company approvals, legal reviews and statement of work (SOW) agreements.

Be sure to identify the roles involved in each activity. This allows the customer's and the salesperson's team to see who is involved. Keep the number of activities brief but thorough. Don't overwhelm the customer. Prominently display the 'Go Live' date so everyone that reviews the plan sees the end date and stays focused on achieving the desired outcome. This helps keep projects on track.

Deliverables required by the team making the decision is a key section. These could be comparison studies, white papers, customer testimonials, references, documents and the like. A good salesperson will help the customer by working to define these early in the process and then modifying the list as additional stakeholders provide their input and requirements.

Mutual action plans can be created in a Word document or spreadsheet, though some good software options exist that are easy to use and produce plans that are easy to update and read. More importantly, they are easy to share and collaborate on

Summary

Fantasy? Fiction? Or commercial reality?

Understanding opportunity management helps a modern salesperson use their resources more effectively. It achieves this by encouraging focus on:

- Qualifying projects or chances to win business

- Assessing competition (including status quo)

- Positioning the offer from a customer perspective

- Understanding who is involved in the decision and how to deliver what they need/want

- Deciding on the best actions to take

- Using mutual action plans to demonstrate competence and drive activity to enable outcomes

As a sales professional, are you actively managing opportunities or relying on random activity and hoping to win business?

10
Leading

S alespeople are change agents, or certainly should start to think and act like this. More often than not, we will be challenging the status quo. We want customers to see things differently and it isn't always easy to do this. The more comfortable we are with change ourselves, the more we can help people manage how they move along their 'change curve'. Then we can then start to talk about change as an opportunity.

Thinking and acting as a 'servant leader' is a role that a modern salesperson can fulfil. A mindset of service to the customer and working to support them and their goal brings in a completely new set of skills, which contribute to an effective hybrid selling approach.

This involves a high degree of customer focus and despite many bold organisational claims it is an area in which many salespeople could do far better. For a number of reasons selling can become self-centred despite the route to modern success being that of taking interest in and helping the customer understand their buying journey.

Becoming a 'servant leader'

Serve to lead

When I left university, I went straight into the commercial world. Some of my friends joined the army. It was while visiting one that I spotted a book on his shelf (not difficult, it was the only one!) called *Serve to Lead*, the original British Army manual on leadership, that he was given at Sandhurst.[15] It struck me as something of a paradox then, but we had important things to do (visit the mess) so did not really discuss it.

Time has passed since then and the concept of 'servant leadership' is something I have spent more time reflecting on, both in its broader context and more specifically on how a salesperson can play the role of a servant leader.

The idea of servant leadership has been around a long time, but it was Robert K Greenleaf in 1970 who coined the term in his essay 'The Servant as Leader':

'A servant-leader focuses primarily on the growth and wellbeing of people and the communities to which they belong. While traditional leadership generally involves the accumulation and exercise of power by one at the "top of the pyramid", servant leadership is different. The servant-leader shares power, puts the needs of others first and helps people develop and perform as highly as possible.'[16]

Essentially, servant leadership principles emphasise facilitation and helping employees grow and harness their maximum potential, empowering both individual team members and the company to be successful. A salesperson should aspire to do this for their customers.

But how can a salesperson be a servant leader when they do not work for the organisation? The answer lies partly in challenging the idea that they do not work for the organisation – they do, or certainly those with a collaborative mindset do. They are just not 'employed' by it. The answer also lies in the concept that a salesperson can adopt the associated traits of servant leadership and help those in a position to apply it in their organisation.

Larry Spears, in his book *Insights on Leadership*, distilled Greenleaf's ideas into ten key servant leadership traits: listening, empathy, stewardship, foresight, persuasion, conceptualisation, awareness, healing, commitment to the growth and development of people and building community.[17]

A well-rounded salesperson will be strong in these characteristics and can play a part in helping key stakeholders apply them in their role. Activities in the sales process can also be tailored to facilitate this for leaders by:

- **Listening** – providing feedback from outside the organisation; this needs to be handled with sensitivity to not jeopardise other relationships

- **Empathy** – using questions effectively can help someone else think from a different perspective: the salesperson is acting as a coach

- **Stewardship** – plans should include proposed use of resources

- **Foresight** – assisting with effective planning

- **Persuasion** – salespeople should be used to preparing coherent arguments based on providing solutions to issues and highlighting benefits; this is an opportunity to share those skills

- **Conceptualisation** – much of a salesperson's role is to guide thinking and build on ideas, so helping others in the process is an extension of this

- **Awareness** – like providing feedback to the organisation this can involve providing individuals information about themselves

- **Healing** – employing conflict management skills

- **Commitment to the growth and development of people** – shared plans can include training and opportunities for individuals in the team to step into larger roles

- **Building community** – salespeople can offer to facilitate or lead project teams; new initiatives can be creatively branded to drive unity

Is this a big ask of salespeople? Maybe. But it is a way of adding value. If they think it is just about providing information those days are gone. As I once heard someone say, 'If that is how you work you might as well get a job as a website'.

Recognising the buying process

Aligning to buying process

More often than ever before, customers are more advanced in their decision making than we realise when they involve salespeople, because huge amounts of information are now available, where previously the salesperson was often the only source.

It pays, then, to take time to try to appreciate where a customer is and align to that. Understanding the steps in the process and the issues that arise helps the salesperson to decide how they can adopt a useful approach in assisting the customer with their decision making. A typical buying process may look like this:

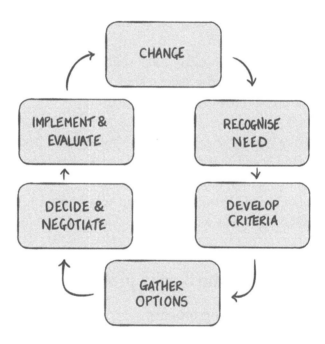

At each stage, a customer may be pondering questions which a salesperson can provide assistance with:

- **Change** – what is different now?

- **Recognise business need** – is it worth doing?

- **Develop criteria** – what do we need to address the issue?

- **Gather and evaluate options** – who offers the best fit?

- **Decide and negotiate** – how can I minimise risk?

- **Implement and evaluate** – was it worth it?

A salesperson can effectively align with customers by recognising where they might benefit from the offering you have and by adapting to fit better to the part of the buying cycle they are currently operating in.

A plate of spaghetti

However, things are rarely that simple. The basic buying process outlined above is really intended more as a conceptual model to help raise a salesperson's awareness. It is unlikely a customer is using a tool like CRM software to track their own progress. They probably don't even know what stage they are at, or indeed that there are different phases they shift through.

In a 2019 report Gartner produced an 'illustrative B2B buying journey'[18] a colleague of mine described it as looking like a plate of spaghetti, and it is fair to say that buying today is a complex activity. Gartner identified that customers need to complete a 'set of jobs' to make a purchase, and that the set involves:

- **Problem identification** – we need to do something.

- **Solution exploration** – what's out there to solve our problem?

- **Requirements building** – what exactly do we need the purchase to do?

- **Supplier selection** – does this do what we want it to do?

- **Validation** – we think we know the right answer, but we need to be sure.

- **Consensus creation** – we need to get everyone on board.

Gartner's buying journey isn't linear – there is a clear understanding that the different activities occurring during the journey are likely to be carried out by customers more than once and may happen concurrently.[19]

Interestingly, the same report showed that customers now spend far less time interacting with suppliers due to the amount of information readily available to them. However, information that makes it easier for customers to navigate their purchasing is valued. Salespeople who focus on helping customers with their buying jobs are much more welcome and likely to be more successful.

Managing change

Change by chance or chance by change?

Understanding change and being able to deal with it can create considerable opportunities for salespeople and customers alike.

'Everything changes and nothing stands still', according to Greek philosopher Heraclitus, known for his doctrine of change being central to the universe. Yet people can fear change and often hide their feelings when they think they are under threat. But change is going to happen anyway, and this can be magnified as the result of implementing sales solutions, things designed to bring business improvements.

To help with this the organisation will need someone spearheading the transition, a leader charged with understanding the change, establishing how it affects people and communicating information to ensure everyone is 'on the journey together'. This is the change agent. An effective change agent acts to smooth the way. As such they may fulfil a number of roles including researcher, trainer, facilitator and counsellor.

Salesperson as change agent

A change agent does not have to work inside the organisation. Indeed, having an external influence can offer fresh and neutral perspectives. As such, it is a role a good salesperson can play, or at least help with.

Acting as an effective change agent a salesperson can:

1. **Know the benefits the changes will bring** – Understand the bigger picture and how the plans for change fit with the company's past, as well as their effect on its future.

2. **Stay in touch with the human side of change** – Even the smallest changes can cause issues to bubble up, and reactions become stronger as the stakes get higher. Change agents must remain visible and listen to people all the time, remaining sensitive to their needs in order to get the most from all concerned.

3. **Balance the people side with a focus on the bottom line** – If they care too much about what everyone thinks, nothing will ever get done. Change agents may have to act tough to ensure overall performance does not suffer. While they take into account people's attitudes and emotions, they still consider more concrete results.

4. **Embody the change** – They appreciate the bigger picture and may not necessarily wait for permission to act – they take risks and expect these to pay off. Above all they show that they are involved as much as anyone else by walking the talk.

5. **Open up the process** – As well as having one
   eye on the results, the change agent will also
   understand how to get there, which includes
   generating ideas with the rest of the team and
   being open to incorporating their knowledge. The
   agent is a catalyst for change, rather than doing all
   the work themselves.

6. **Remember what is great about the business
   already** – Organisations rely on a degree of
   stability, so the old ways should not all be
   abandoned entirely for the allure of 'shiny
   new things'. The change agent must manage
   continuity, valuing stability in the face of all this
   other change.

Using the 'change curve'

Everyone handles change differently, with different emotions at play at different times. I encourage
salespeople to bear in mind the Kübler-Ross
Change Curve™[20] to understand the internal emotional journey that people typically experience
when dealing with change and transition. Applying
this concept to customers, the stages of such a journey may include shock and denial, frustration and
anger, bargaining and exploration, depression, and
acceptance and commitment.

Shock and denial – People can be stunned that something has happened and may not be able to digest

that they need to change and adapt to something new. They may need time to adjust and not accept that they should do anything.

Helping customers understand why something is happening and how it can be helpful is the approach salespeople should take. It is all about communication, though care should be taken not to provide too much information too quickly, to avoid overwhelming the customer. This is a common mistake salespeople make, as they are not experiencing the same emotion; indeed they may be excited and want to move things forward as the benefits are clear to them.

Frustration and anger – As reality sets in so can fear of what lies ahead. This in turn can become resentment. Realising that the future requires a shift out of their comfort zone can make people angry at the learning and adapting required.

This needs salespeople to use a high level of sensitivity as people can vent their anger in different ways. It is best to plan well for this and use the plans to continue communication and provide support. This is a natural stage and will pass but trying to push it too fast can cause extra problems.

Bargaining and exploration – When people finally understand the change and realise how they must adapt to new situations and circumstances, they may try to find the best possible scenario for them to fit in and adapt to. They will try to compromise.

A salesperson should ensure that everyone gets the best information so that they can deal with changes effectively. Necessary training and implementation schedules need to be planned and applied. It is important not to try to rush this stage or expect outcomes to be delivered in full immediately.

Depression – If no compromise has been possible, it is not unusual for people to feel 'The worst has happened; and *they* don't listen to me, anyway'. This will pass; the only way to deal with it is patience.

Acceptance and commitment – People finally begin to embrace the change, accept the situation and start building new aspirations. They understand the importance of the change and work towards it.

This is when the benefits of hard work begin to become clear, so salespeople should highlight these and try to amplify them. If some results have already been achieved this is a cause for celebration, and even if it is just a case that the potential is now more tangible then this should be used to drive activity.

The key to success in many sales scenarios is adaptability and this model provides an excellent means to recognise what do and when.

Combating VUCA

The original VUCA model

VUCA is a concept originally used by the US military. It was coined to describe the environment after the Cold War when threats were considered to come from different sources that were harder to track, could appear and then disappear and that were highly confusing. It describes a landscape of volatility, uncertainty, complexity and ambiguity.

More recently, VUCA has been used to inform leadership and also to provide solid thinking that salespeople can use. In the commercial world the concept of VUCA can be considered a means of identifying opportunities. Focusing on each element separately helps determine better ways of working to respond to change.

Volatility – Any market is volatile, and the kind of volatility will reflect on the organisation. In highly volatile industries or markets it can be hard for business to keep up.

Uncertainty – How confidently can your customer predict what might impact on their business? How much do they really know (or can you find out) about the environment they operate in? The more sophisticated the market, the harder it is to predict anything.

Complexity – How many factors does your customer need to take into account, and what networks link (or separate) them? A tangled network can be difficult to analyse.

Ambiguity – How clearly can your customer explain the factors that affect their business? What might conflict with or confuse these explanations? It can be hard to read the signs and know what is relevant.

VUCA Prime

Introduced in 2007 by Robert Johansen, VUCA Prime[21] offers a model for cutting through and neutralising each element of VUCA, using positive approaches, such as:

Vision to counter Volatility – stay focused. While experiencing change, focusing on the goal should help keep stakeholders' attention on shared purpose and potential benefits.

Understanding to cut through Uncertainty – use different ways and provide insight to increase understanding of the factors that are confusing the situation.

Clarity to cut down Complexity – make plans and messages simple and clear so decisions become easier and lead to quicker implementation.

Agility to outflank Ambiguity – develop the ability to adapt. When presented with alternatives, be able to make an adjustment to an approach that will drive the desired outcome better than the original plan.

In an ever-changing world, a salesperson equipped with a good understanding of VUCA Prime can bring great value in making sense of this. Navigating in a VUCA environment should not be seen as a problem that can be resolved but as an ongoing scenario that must be effectively managed.

To survive and thrive, organisations need to consider many kinds of input when making strategic decisions in a VUCA environment. They need to be proactive, not reactive: and good salespeople can help them.

VUCA Prime as a sales model

Sales is shifting more than ever before towards using a more collaborative approach, so an effective sales-person can position themselves as something of a resource to their customers.

Using the VUCA Prime sales model helps do this by giving focus to both self and others. It allows sales-people to prepare to act confidently then guide customers more effectively. Time spent to pause and reflect will be invaluable to all parties, as it means activity to make appropriate changes heads in the right direction with clearly defined steps.

Best practice salespeople can use includes:

- **Vision**
  - Defining goals/targets/objectives

- Clarifying purpose and ambition

- Establishing mutual benefit

- Recognising that inputs drive outputs

- **Understanding**

  - Listening and getting to know the customer

  - Generating insight

  - Applying structured thinking models (like five whys or fishbone diagrams)

  - Telling stories

- **Clarity**

  - Acting with courage

  - Defining steps and KPIs

  - Creative thinking (including models like six thinking hats or SCAMPER)

- **Agility**

  - Becoming more adaptable

  - Using 'OODA loops' (observe–orient–decide–act)

  - Applying an entrepreneurial mindset

This might sound like a big ask, but the rewards are large, too. Never have the changes and associated challenges been so dramatic. The opportunity to genuinely achieve 'trusted adviser' status to which many salespeople aspire is clear and present.

Summary

Lead the way.

A salesperson that can bring leadership skills to their approach is able to provide value in a different form for their customers. It is an up-to-the-minute way of working that goes way beyond being a 'purveyor of fine information'. That is most likely already out there, and the customer has probably already consumed it.

When a salesperson can bring their skills to bear and help a customer to use what is available, that is when they will make a difference.

To do this involves:

- Acting as a servant leader
- Focusing on assisting with buying journeys
- Understanding and facilitating change
- Using VUCA Prime to structure thinking and develop a joint approach

Are you perceived as a leader and guide by your customers?

11
Value Selling

Selling based on value is not particularly new. There has been a focus on this since the early 2000s. However, that does not make it any less important now. As salespeople, we really have got to understand what value is. But, as a colleague of mine often says, 'It's a mystery'.

We don't really know what value is. We have got to work out what it is *to the customer*. That is the secret of value selling. Once we know how we can start to define this with customers, then we can start to bring the insights and ways of working that are going to help them. We work to discover what value is, then start to create and to deliver on that.

This presents a whole set of sales skills and techniques which a modern salesperson should be comfortable with to be able to make a difference to their customer and be successful in the present sales environment.

It's a mystery

What is value?

The answer is key to understanding value selling, so it makes sense to first define what value means. *The Oxford English Dictionary* helps with this by stating it is 'The regard that something is held to deserve; the importance, worth, or usefulness of something'.

However, I like the response that value selling expert Mike Wilkinson often gives, which is 'It's a mystery'.[22] I like it as, though initially it appears to be rather unhelpful, it is a perfect starting point from which a salesperson can approach value selling. The mystery is in the fact that though we might have a nice tidy dictionary definition and even an idea as a salesperson what our customers will probably value in our offer, we cannot be totally sure.

It's rather like 'beauty is in the eye of the beholder'. The whole point of value selling is to understand the customer and what they value so that the proposition can be tailored to match. It is essentially about what a salesperson can do for the customer and their business.

Based on business outcomes

Using this concept, we could describe value selling as an approach that aims to quantify the value or worth that your solution delivers to a customer in terms relevant to them and their business. It involves concentrating on the impact that what you do will have for them, or the business advantages they may enjoy as a result of employing your solution. In a competitive world, it also means highlighting your advantages when compared with those of competing products and services.

The wise man built his house...

There is a song we sang at school about a wise man who built his house on rock and when it rained the house stood firm. Conversely, the foolish man built his house on sand and when it rained it was washed away. The relevance of this to value selling? Solid foundations.

Value selling, as the name suggests, is selling a value that both buyer and seller see as higher than that in more 'traditional' forms of selling. The complexity is also greater, so a strong foundation in sales essentials is a prerequisite. It would be difficult to be successful in this more involved style of selling without a solid background in the basics.

The challenge of value

Breaking down activity

In his book *The Seven Challenges of Value* Mike Wilkinson explores understanding, creating and delivering value.[23] This is an excellent guide for sales-people, and indeed organisations, who are involved in value selling. He recognises the big challenge this can present and breaks it down into more manageable chunks – seven challenges:

1. Understanding just what value is

2. Recognising that value and value perceptions are constantly changing

3. Identifying people who care about value

4. Differentiating in ways that matter

5. Communicating your value

6. Capturing your value through price

7. Delivering the value you promise

Let's look at the these in a little more detail…

Challenge No. 1: Understand what value is.

This can be broken into three parts:

- Value as a concept

- What value means to our customers (as our understanding of value and theirs might differ)

- Making sure that everyone in our business understands value in the same way

Essentially, this helps us recognise that *customers* define value, not salespeople or marketers. The skill is to really understand the customer's perception of what is valuable.

Mike has developed the 'value triad' to help salespeople structure their thinking more effectively. It focuses on where value can be created. This could be through:

- **Revenue gain** – how can our product or service help our customer improve their revenues?

- **Cost reduction** – how can our product or service help our customer reduce their costs?

- **Emotional contribution** – how do they make decisions?

The first two are tangible, objective measures against which a real monetary value can be calculated. However, if you do not know how your customer generates revenue or how they incur costs, this is going to be difficult. If you can uncover the answer to these and your competitors cannot, you are beginning to develop an advantage over them.

The third component is much more intangible and subjective, but while human beings are making decisions, it is very important. This is the value of trust, confidence, the brand, the relationships, ease of doing business, cultural fit and generally 'feeling good' when doing business with you.

Understanding the elements of the value triad helps salespeople understand value for each customer. However, everyone in the sales organisation should understand value as a concept, and what it means to each customer. If they don't know, how will they understand their role in creating and delivering customer value?

Challenge No 2: Recognise that a customer's value perceptions are constantly changing.

This requires you to keep close and up to date with what is happening with the customer and how it affects their thinking. Elements such as economic impacts, changing internal priorities, personnel turnover, political considerations, regulatory issues and more can influence and change value perceptions.

Challenge No 3: Identify and talk to people who care the most about your value.

Firstly, you can't sell value to people, or organisations, that don't care about value.

Also, as today's decision-making processes become increasingly more complex, we need to win over those people who can really see and appreciate the value we can deliver. These people will then act as our influencers inside the organisation. Most salespeople will not be present when the decision to buy (or not) is made. So, they must be sure that the sales message and associated value is communicated effectively internally. This is helped by understanding *who* makes the decision and *how* it is made.

Challenge No 4: Differentiate your offering.

Being different is NOT differentiation. You must be different in ways that are important to the customer. In other words, you must recognise what they value and try to calculate that.

Challenge No 5: Communicate your value.

Customers don't want vague promises, they want firm commitments. They don't want to know you can save them money or make them money. They want to know how much and by when. Creating a powerful and persuasive value proposition is critical.

Top salespeople work on the premise of having to create two value propositions. The first is at the beginning of the sales process. This should answer the question 'Why should I talk to you?' The second, more focused, value proposition is presented at the end and answers the question 'Why should we choose you?' Joining the two together are the activities involved in value-based selling.

Building a powerful, persuasive, final value proposition is important and should have three key components:

- The customer can clearly see that your solution addresses their issues.

- The customer can see that you offer things they cannot get elsewhere (or at least not done as well).

- The customer not only hears a good story, but you can prove that you can do the things you say you can do.

Take just one of the components away and the strength of the proposition is seriously affected.

Challenge No 6: Capturing your value through price.

The concept of the 'the negotiation corridor' helps us establish price. This is the difference between the maximum price you could charge to deliver your value, and the price the customer is currently paying (or the price they would pay if they did not choose your solution). All work up to now has been designed to help make that negotiation corridor as wide as possible by truly understanding the things that are important to your customer.

Remember that price itself is NOT the reason customers do not buy. They do not buy because they do not see the value in the offer.

Challenge No 7: Deliver your value.

This takes us right back to the beginning. Does everyone in the sales organisation really understand their role in understanding, creating and delivering customer value to this customer?

Assuming they do – and that is some assumption – the next task is delivering AND measuring the value you promised. So, you need to focus on your value and your performance.

Make sure the customer is getting the value you promised. If they are, constantly remind them – because customers have a great ability to forget things like that. If they are not, address the issues and put things right, because customers have a great ability to remember and make issues of having been let down.

Finally, identify opportunities for creating and delivering even more value for the customer by understanding them in ever greater detail. Success and understanding lead to more opportunities.

Generating insight

You've got another think coming

Yes, you have. Think. Contrary to popular opinion – and the Judas Priest song – it is 'think', not 'thing'.

Most people would still understand the meaning of the expression as being something like 'you're mistaken'. And this is a mistake salespeople can make when trying to add value by fixing problems and giving information.

If a salesperson believes they are adding value by throwing lots of different things at a customer, this is a mistake. Quite often, being on the end of 'another thing coming' can be overwhelming for the customer. It is poor selling to use this type of shotgun approach, hoping to eventually hit with something of relevance that the customer must work out for themselves.

A more sophisticated way of selling, that is more valuable to the customer, is to give them 'another think coming'. This is not to tell them they are wrong, but to use provocative questions grounded in insight developed in preparation to make them think. A salesperson looking to create value should spend time in this sort of discussion. To be effective the questions should be prepared and crafted from an understanding of the various factors at play.

One of the best things a salesperson can hear is 'that's a good question' or 'you've really made me think'. It tends not to happen by accident.

Making thinks come

So, what can salespeople do?

Well, the answer is partly what they should not do, and that is solve problems.

That might seem a little counterintuitive, as surely selling is all about problem solving. And to a degree it is, but the best salespeople go about this in a slightly different way to the standard 'see problem, fix problem' approach that many adopt.

As customers are increasingly in a better position to sort out their own issues, just giving an answer they already know does not add any value. It could also be that the customer doesn't recognise they have an issue and then gets confused and frustrated when salespeople talk about things which seem irrelevant to them.

When salespeople really make an impression on customers is when they can give a new perspective on the customer's own world: when they can shine a light on an issue, make sense of something that is confusing or provide a means to help a customer succeed. This is when they start to make a difference.

It is often about looking at the bigger picture and, by making an effort to understand and share this with a more collaborative approach, a salesperson can set themselves apart and position themselves as a valuable resource for the customer. By getting to grips with and helping the customer to focus on what is really going on, the nature of the relationship changes and becomes one that can generate much more value for all parties.

This, however, takes skill and an understanding of how to do what this involves. Too many salespeople have their heads filled with information about their products and services rather than being equipped to deal with what customers really care about. Is it surprising, then, that many customers now say that they would prefer to buy without any interaction with salespeople as they are simply not getting anything from that dialogue?

We are talking about a more sophisticated way of selling, and this is what customers are demanding. There is no point in turning up and telling them what they already know. But preparing to provide information and ask questions that really make someone think is when great steps can be made.

Summary

'That was really valuable.'

One of the best things a salesperson can hear at the end of an interaction with a customer is praise for having helped the customer with their thinking. Selling value is not about being prescriptive and firing off solutions as soon as any inkling of a problem is detected. It is about exploration and understanding. Those who understand *that* are the most successful. They do this by:

- Defining what value means for the customer

- Positioning what they can do in a way that is meaningful in relation to the customer's definition

- Generating insight to drive discussion that explores ways a customer can benefit

- Pricing and negotiating based on outcomes for the customer

As a sales professional are you having 'valuable value discussions' or do you move too quickly into 'solution mode'?

12
Expand

'Land and expand' is a model often talked about. Some people have a bit of a problem with this because it sounds a bit manipulative. But it makes sense. It is about starting a project, finding some initial opportunities, delivering on those and helping the customer achieve something relevant to them. Consequently, the whole relationship naturally starts to grow. From this point of view, expansion is not a bad thing. It makes a lot of sense. It is what both parties want and where account management comes into play.

Among other things, good account management involves building on the elements used in opportunity management and applying these and the associated thinking to keep building the relationship by defining value, scoping success and delivering the outcomes that we promise to customers.

Accordingly, the discipline of customer success management (CSM) is something that salespeople should understand. The need to appreciate this developing function, as a means to ensure the customer gets what we promise to deliver, is vital. While already very popular in the IT sector, CSM is also starting to be used in other areas. It can bring another dimension to the way a salesperson can position themselves and their solutions.

Perhaps above all else a salesperson needs to be strong in self-management. With so many demands on today's seller the ability to make decisions and give focus to things that have an impact is key. In a role that can be quite pressured and stressful good physical and mental health can also play an important part in an individual's ability to perform.

Account management

More than a title?

A LinkedIn search lists over 14,000,000 people with 'account manager' in their title.

It makes me wonder whether they actually undertake that role or whether it is one given to appease them and/or customers. Perhaps I am being a little cynical but I wonder if all these positions are about growth and developing business proactively or whether they are more 'order taker', transactional, roles. I know it is a source of frustration for many 'real' account managers who feel their role is belittled when the title is given away so freely.

Another area that frustrates account managers is when organisations seem to miss the point that this is about managing existing customer relationships and is focused on creating long-term and profitable partnerships. Instead, the account manager ends up fighting fires and performing tasks that need doing but which ideally other parts of the organisation should be covering, to allow them to focus on revenue and retention.

Special skill set

Is this just selling though?

Well, it is the 'same but different'. Some skills for account management need to be developed. However, as the hybrid selling approach grows so does the need for salespeople to grow their competence in the areas associated with good account management. The main ones to consider are:

1. **Communication** – This needs to be good in sales anyway but those with greater account management responsibilities often need to

communicate with different people at different levels. It is necessary to be in touch with a variety of stakeholders, both internal and external. This means an ability to flex between communicating to different personality styes, as well as to understand individuals' key drivers.

2. **Alignment** – Salespeople must be expert in what their company does and also what the customer does, so they can then tailor solutions that align those goals. This entails facilitating working together towards mutually beneficial outcomes. Recognising, accepting and valuing the interdependent nature of the relationship plays a key part in this.

3. **Strategic thinking** – Building strong relationships often needs a more strategic perspective. For account managers, the goals tend to be longer-term, not just chasing short-term sales figures. The focus tends to be on what the organisations are trying to achieve at a broader business level.

4. **Leading** – Modern salespeople need to be able to lead customers. They should aspire to guide the customer and help them make decisions. This is not about manipulating but assisting and encouraging the customer to do what is right for them. The same leadership skills will be used with colleagues.

5. **Negotiation** – An important skill for all sales-people, and certainly for an account manager.

They are likely to be negotiating on a regular basis, though not just on the terms and conditions of a contract. Quite often they will be involved in problem-solving discussions and even managing conflict.

6. **Focus** – More specifically, results focus. Account managers have a responsibility to make sure their organisation delivers value to all parties and to drive the activities to achieve this. After all, this is why the customer remains an 'account'.

Warwick Brown, founder of KAM Club (a great resource if you want to understand more about specific account management skills) talks about 'getting out of the position of supplier', by which he is indicating that your ambition should be to move on from being viewed as someone 'providing', on a transactional basis, and become a longer-term, genuine 'trusted adviser'.[24] I like this thinking, especially as it infers that the customer is the one who bestows the trusted adviser status.

Customer success management

CSM is a discipline that is closely related to sales. As a profession it is still in its infancy, but it is growing and maturing rapidly. It is about anticipating customer challenges and proactively providing solutions before the need is perceived, thereby helping to improve customer happiness and retention, and increasing revenue and customer loyalty.

Customer 'success' is different from customer 'support' though they are very much linked:

- Customer support focuses on working reactively on the front lines as the function that solves problems when customers raise them.

- Customer success is focused on working proactively in partnership with customers to help them get more value out of their purchase; it drives the customer experience forward and has a higher degree of future orientation.

The benefit of understanding this discipline is that CSM activity is essentially about delivering customer outcomes. This should also be top of a salesperson's mind.

Driving wider adoption

CSM is a concept, and indeed a role, that originated in the IT/technology space. Effective adoption of solutions is key to ongoing sales and while this may seem pretty simple to measure – for instance, how many times a user 'logs on' – in reality there is far more to it. It is important to connect the dots between adoption and value.

Therefore, salespeople are encouraged to recognise the drivers behind every purchase, and the outcomes customers are seeking to achieve – whether increased productivity, reduced risk, improvements to how they sell or something else entirely unique to their business. Effective adoption should be measured by the customer's definition of success, not yours. You want them to use your product, sure, but it's more important that they see real value in using it. If you can show them you understand how they operate and how what you contribute can help them achieve their business targets, you will make a difference.

The Cisco model

Tech giant Cisco are strong advocates of a robust approach to CSM and have developed their own model for delivering long-term success in this way.[25] It is worth briefly covering their approach.

The five steps in Cisco's process are:

1. **Validate**: Establish what the customer values and sees as success, and understand why they made the decision to purchase, who made the decision, what their KPIs were and what they hope the purchase will do *for them*.

2. **Enable awareness**: Customers only value what they use and use from choice (not just because

they bought it). They are more likely to choose your product or service if they know how it will help them do *what they want to do*.

3. **Build the customer's learning**: Different people within the business will have different needs and expectations, and you must address each person's needs to make them choose (rather than just use) what you sell. Some key people may need (or value) extra training or support material.

4. **Enable usage**: Show how the solution meets the customer's definition of success. If you can, monitor usage regularly to identify areas for improvement or training needs. Help the customer show their management in their own words how what you sold them helped them achieve KPIs.

5. **Embed usage**: Demonstrate how key features of your solution can be embedded in the customer's internal processes. This helps bridge the gap between 'use' and 'choose' and creates future opportunities.

It is very much about understanding the customer, working with them and helping them to achieve. This is what professional selling is about today.

Self-management

Managing time

I love a good sci-fi film involving time travel. *Back to the Future* is a classic and the *Bill and Ted* films are excellent. But 'time management' is more than just managing oneself and using that most valuable of resources – time – intelligently. 'Self-management' is a far more accurate term.

It is a hot topic in training, as many salespeople know they could be better at it and appreciate the difference it makes to their productivity. Like 'closing', they often seek a magic bullet, but as with closing there isn't one, and it is down to doing a series of things well. I break down the concept and key activities to give people a structure to manage themselves and their decision-making better, for this is what really makes the difference.

The process of understanding how to make better decisions about time and other valuable resources is based on understanding these key elements:

1. **Purpose** – What are you here for? Not in an existential or deep way (though taking time to tie things back to values and personal drivers does make sense, as that creates a far more powerful desire to act). In the time we have available we

focus on our aims and on our role; to use another word, 'objectives'.

2. **Roles and responsibilities** – What do you do? Essentially, how should your job be defined, and what do you need to do to achieve your objectives?

3. **Activities** – What do you actually do? This considers 'a day in the life'. A list of all the tasks actually performed can usually uncover things that do not contribute to achieving objectives: stop doing them.

4. **Priorities** – What should you be doing and when? Now we get down to the bit many people find difficult, using their time most effectively. This is based on an understanding of 'urgent' and 'important'.

   - 'Urgent' means 'the closer to the deadline the more urgent': simple, not to be confused with

   - 'Important', which is based on impact: the greater the contribution to achieving objectives then the more important something is.

'Urgent' and 'important' often get confused and this is when people make poor choices in using their time. Understanding the difference and defining tasks and how to undertake them is how we can really make a difference: assign your tasks to one of four categories.

Important AND urgent

Two types of task are often found in this category: ones that could not have been foreseen, and others that have been left until the last minute.

Eliminate last-minute activities by planning ahead and avoiding procrastination, and leave time available to handle unexpected issues and unplanned but important activities.

Not important AND not urgent

These trivial activities are just a distraction – avoid them if possible.

You can often simply ignore or cancel many of them; often nobody notices. However, there may be activities that other people want you to do, even though they don't contribute to your objective. A polite 'no' and short explanation usually works. That you are focusing on customer-facing activity is enough reason for most people.

Not important BUT urgent

These are things that prevent you from achieving your goals. Try to reschedule or delegate.

Other people often generate these tasks. Sometimes it is appropriate to say 'no' (politely), or to encourage people to solve the problem themselves. Alternatively, try to have time slots when you are available to deal with people. This can be tough for salespeople but doing this allows you to concentrate on important activities (like writing proposals or prospecting) for longer and ultimately better results.

Important BUT not urgent

These are the activities that help you achieve your personal and professional goals.

Schedule plenty of time to do these things properly, so that they do not become urgent. Planning and blocking out this time help us stay on track and avoid unnecessary stress.

The theory is simple though the application can be harder, particularly as trivial activities are often fun and/or easy and urgent but not important requests from senior people that need tact to manage.

Wellness matters

All of us risk challenging our mental health and well-being during our careers and life. But the world of sales amplifies this risk, with research showing poor mental health and stress-related illness are three times more likely among salespeople. Couple that with 67% of salespeople saying they have experienced burnout, or feel they might burn out soon.[26]

It makes sense; missing targets, facing rejection daily and suspecting that everyone is doing better than you can make you feel like you want the ground to swallow you up. What can be a tough environment leaves your sales professional's mental wellbeing and mindset under constant strain.

Telling people to just talk more about their mental health isn't enough any more. Instead, we need to focus on promoting prevention, early intervention and coping mechanisms. I interviewed Chris Hatfield of Sales Psyche, who shared great advice on this important topic:[27]

- To take away the stressors that can build up, use socialising such as meeting friends, going to the gym, visiting the office and generally being with people

- Practise positive 'self-talk' and eliminate the internal dialogue around harmful or limiting beliefs that can become a self-fulfilling prophecy

- Avoid perfectionism and other ways the 'impostor syndrome' can manifest itself including workaholism and feeling required to be expert in everything

- Identify the emotional triggers that signal the potential for higher stress and challenge what prompts them (are real causes for concern behind them?)

- Reset unhelpful emotions and associated thinking by taking time to step back and assess

Recognising the signs of stress and burnout is key, though not always easy to do.

Burnout can take away people's emotions and enthusiasm and leave them feeling helpless and hopeless; but they might just appear disengaged. A highly stressed person, on the other hand, can look highly engaged because of the hyper nature of their activity.

Sales leaders must accept responsibility to be more aware of their subordinates' mental wellbeing, if not for humane reasons then for the massive impact it can have on productivity and success. Ways to improve their awareness may be to:

- Create a space to check and ask about people's wellbeing using questions like 'On a scale where one's bad and ten's great, how are you doing?' and 'What's on your mind?'

- Build better relationships with their team, to be able to discuss things more freely

- Practise what they preach; understand and use mindful techniques

- Offer support

With the amount some organisations invest in the 'tech stack' to support salespeople with intelligence to perform the job more effectively, it seems crazy that the most important type of intelligence is often ignored. Without doubt what Sales Psyche and similar organisations offer can make a real difference for any professional sales set-up.

Daily reflection habit

A habit I have developed is that of daily reflection.

First thing in the morning I think about the day ahead, as this helps me construct positive intentions and understand the emotional tone for what lies ahead. I find that by doing this I am more likely to deliver on the things I have planned. I aim to own the day and stay on track; starting off in the right direction helps.

Reflecting on the outcome of the day helps me learn by becoming more aware of the challenges I face for personal growth and my career.

I use a coaching chat bot driven by AI (called Rocky), as I like the way the questions it asks stimulate my thinking. I also like being able to switch the growth path I am on for what I feel to be most relevant at the time. Modules Rocky offers include Clarity, Discipline, Communication, People and Wellbeing.

Perhaps 'talking to a robot' isn't for everyone, but there are many different ways to achieve the same benefits. Some of my colleagues swear by journaling, others by meditation. Mindfulness is a practice that is also growing in popularity. Even setting a little time aside to read something has a positive effect. It is all about creating a good habit.

This style of quiet thinking might not be for everyone and some may question the time involved. But it does not have to take long and the benefits are worth it, as the small changes start to add up to make a difference to performance. Ways to develop a more 'active' approach to reflection could include:

- Using a 'review buddy', a friend or colleague who can listen and ask questions

- Making a list, a very basic form of journaling, in which you note 'what went well today' and 'what would I do differently' and circle action points

- Creating a mind map or even drawing a little picture to represent the day: this stimulates the mind and sets you thinking

- Asking questions, which should be natural to a salesperson so, rather than try to answer them, ask them: your brain will look for answers

- Future scoping: some people prefer to look forwards rather than backwards; since this should be a skill salespeople are competent in it makes sense to use it for personal benefit, too.

Learning and developing new ways of working takes practice before results will show. Using some form of reflection can help with that process and with focus on personal improvement.

Let's get physical

Not a big section on this as the 'healthy body, healthy mind' mantra is well known. So, let's keep it to:

- Do some exercise

- Eat well

- Drink more… water!

You know the drills.

All three will make a difference, as selling can be quite a demanding job, so being physically fit makes sense.

Summary

It is important to have a growth mindset.

Good salespeople tend to have a more natural inclination towards growth. They have a growth mindset which means they continue to learn and put the effort into getting better.

Someone with a growth mindset sees mistakes as learning opportunities and looks for feedback. Those with a fixed mindset believe their abilities are innate and cannot be changed. They may also believe that talent and intelligence alone lead to success, and that effort is not required. Sadly, we come across this mindset too often with salespeople.

Whether for business with a customer or for themselves as an individual, growth is always on the mind of the best sales professionals. Ways to achieve this include:

- Using good account management practices

- Building relationships with customers

- Focusing on customer success and delivering results

- Employing self-management techniques to focus on high-impact activity

- Keeping well – physically and mentally

- Reflecting on how to develop personally

- Are you doing everything you can to be the best for your customers and yourself?

PART 3
PERSONAL EVOLUTION

What are you going to do about it?

This book, like selling, is about action. While it is all very well discussing what we could, would and should do, we need to make that into what we *will* do.

This part is designed to give you an understanding of how *you* rate in the core elements of hybrid selling so that you can develop actions to become more effective. It is intended to help you make things happen to get maximum benefit from understanding and using a modern approach to selling.

13
Understanding Yourself

This book is all about hybrid selling and I am sure you are interested in how you measure up on the various competencies involved. This is not a massive assumption to make: I know from years as a trainer that the self-discovery parts of the course are always popular; why else would you be reading this book?

Accordingly, I have developed a self-assessment tool you can use to establish where you are now and how you can start to develop these skills.

Instructions for taking the self-assessment

The self-assessment consists of six sections that reflect the six elements of the EVOLVE model for hybrid selling. Each has ten statements for you to consider.

EXAMPLE – ESSENTIALS

This worked example shows how one salesperson answered the questions in the Essentials section of the self-assessment (see next section) and how they calculated their score for this part of the EVOLVE framework.

	Always		Often			Sometimes			Never		
	10	9	8	7	6	5	4	3	2	1	
I use a structured basis to assess whether potential business is a good fit for both parties					✓						
I consider whether (and how) prospects are likely to collaborate			✓								
I know what value looks like for a customer and the reasons why we work together						✓					
I identify and map the stakeholders for an opportunity and consider what is important to them		✓									
My meetings are well prepared and structured			✓								
I ask considered and insightful questions				✓							
I use a well-developed and structured proposal format rather than just a quote							✓				
My presentations put the customer first							✓				
I run regular and scheduled reviews that focus on the value the customer is getting		✓									
My approach is based on trying to be a good partner to all customers				✓							
Total		18	16	14	6	5	8				67%

Your self-assessment

Essentials

Essentials for success are the foundation of all selling. Without these there is nothing to build on and it is difficult to become proficient in the other areas required to use an effective hybrid approach.

	Always			Often		Sometimes			Never		
	10	9	8	7	6	5	4	3	2	1	
I use a structured basis to assess whether potential business is a good fit for both parties											
I consider whether (and how) prospects are likely to collaborate											
I know what value looks like for a customer and the reasons why we work together											
I identify and map the stakeholders for an opportunity and consider what is important to them											
My meetings are well prepared and structured											
I ask considered and insightful questions											
I use a well-developed and structured proposal format rather than just a quote											
My presentations put the customer first											
I run regular and scheduled reviews that focus on the value the customer is getting											
My approach is based on trying to be a good partner to all customers											
Total											

Virtual selling

How I use technology to make selling more effective. Includes skill in online meetings and collaboration, use of video, social selling and an appreciation of AI and its applications.

	Always		Often			Sometimes			Never	
	10	9	8	7	6	5	4	3	2	1
Mentally, I treat virtual meetings as if they are an in-person meeting										
I have a good technical set-up (video, audio, lighting, background) for virtual meetings										
I use tools to help me present and collaborate online (eg whiteboards)										
I am comfortable recording video and sending it to customers										
I am comfortable posting video to social media										
My LinkedIn profile looks good (banner, picture, features, posts and full CV)										
My LinkedIn summary is customer-centric and focuses on their challenges										
I post and comment regularly on business-related social media										
I am conscious of and deliberately build my personal brand										
I use technology to make my life easier										
Total										

Opportunity management

How I use tools and techniques to progress specific projects or chances to win identified pieces of business from current accounts or from new customers.

	Always		Often			Sometimes			Never		
	10	9	8	7	6	5	4	3	2	1	
I have a system and structure for progressing projects and opportunities											
I use defined criteria to qualify what makes a good opportunity											
I capture information, identifying what I know and don't know											
I identify different types of stakeholder to inform my sales approach											
I map decision-making units (DMUs) as a normal activity for any opportunity											
I involve others in collating information and planning next steps											
Next steps to progress and win an opportunity are clearly stated											
I use mutual action plans to map out and enable outcomes for customers											
I share mutual action plans, using a software option											
I conduct win/lose reviews with colleagues and customers											
Total											

Leading

I understand why and how to guide customers ethically, to help them address challenges and make better decisions. I use principles of 'servant leadership' to drive better combined outcomes.

	Always		Often			Sometimes			Never		
	10	9	8	7	6	5	4	3	2	1	
I believe my role is about helping customers to buy											
I use my skills to guide customers to achieve their maximum potential											
The customer's buying process is a key consideration in how I work											
I know what customers must achieve to make progress on their buying journey											
Status quo is my main competition; I am prepared to lead and manage change											
I understand and use change strategy models											
People consider me a valuable resource when they are making decisions											
I am comfortable challenging others about their thinking											
I often get asked my opinion by both colleagues and customers											
I set an example and 'walk the talk'											
Total											

Value selling

I understand, and can define and communicate, value aligned to the customer's interests.

	Always		Often			Sometimes			Never		
	10	9	8	7	6	5	4	3	2	1	
I ask questions to learn and discover ways to improve things for my customers											
I recognise that value is ultimately defined by the customer											
I actively seek to help my customer find a better way to do something											
Customers' emotional and personal drivers inform my determination of value											
I keep aware of people's changing perceptions of value											
I am deliberate in how I try to generate insight for customers											
Information I share is selective and curated with the customer in mind											
My pricing reflects the value a customer derives from my offer											
I defend or negotiate prices with value at the centre of the discussion											
I regularly review with customers the value they are receiving working with us											
Total											

Expanding

I look for ways to grow business through developing relationships and delivering outcomes. Involves good account management and customer success practices.

	Always		Often		Sometimes		Never			
	10	9	8	7	6	5	4	3	2	1
I arrange feedback calls with all customers										
I take a strategic perspective when I talk to customers about longer-term plans										
If mistakes are made I put them right, move on and try not to get stuck in the past										
I recognise that customer success will drive future business and act accordingly										
I regularly contact customers with useful things, even if not currently on projects										
I structure my day/week to be as productive as possible										
I make my decisions based on deadlines and how an activity will impact on my goals										
I can say 'no' to people										
I try to keep myself fit and well										
I schedule time every day to think about how I can become a better salesperson										
Total										

Think about each statement and award yourself a mark on a scale from 10 ('I always do this') to 1 ('I never do this') to reflect how accurately the statement reflects what you actually do (rather than what you plan to do, or try to do).

Add up the sum of each of the columns: for example, if there are three responses in column '7' (Often), score 3 x 7 = 21 for that column.

Add the score for each column to get your overall percentage for that EVOLVE element. (If you score 100%, retake the test and remember that honesty is a key part of professional selling, and that starts with being honest to yourself!)

You can plot your scores on the 'Hybrid Selling Radar'. This is useful if you like to process information visually.

For your overall hybrid selling score take the total scores for each of the EVOLVE elements and sum. Divide by six and round to the nearest whole number to find your overall score. For example:

Essentials =	63
Virtual selling =	70
Opportunity management =	58
Leading =	78
Value selling =	69
Expanding =	72
SUM =	410
divided by 6 =	68.333
rounded to nearest whole number =	**68**

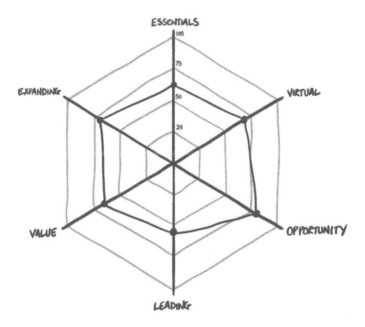

Invest time to reflect on what you may have learned from the self-assessment. The questions in the 'Interpretation' section at the end of this chapter will help.

My hybrid selling score:

Essentials =

Virtual selling =

Opportunity management =

Leading =

Value selling =

Expanding =

SUM =   – – – – – – – – – – – –

divided by 6 and rounded =

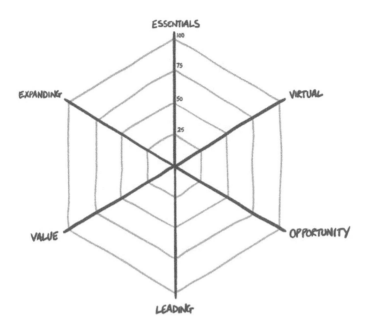

Interpretation

The self-assessment can be used to predict which of the six elements of hybrid selling you may have difficulty bringing into your sales approach. For example, if you ranked the statements regarding 'Leading' low, you may have difficulty in understanding the way people buy or guide customers to make better decisions.

This, in turn, helps you diagnose which of your hybrid selling skills you may want to consider strengthening. If you scored low, for example, in 'Opportunity management' and there seems to be an issue in the way you approach more complex projects, you may want to examine ways that you structure the information you hold about the customer and your understanding of them, to develop a more planned and controlled way of working.

Keep in mind that a high score alone does not guarantee successful hybrid selling; equally, a low score does not mean you will never succeed in adopting the skills to be successful. Indeed, very high or low scores can distort how a salesperson thinks about themselves.

It's all connected

While each element is important, if you are lacking in one part then, because of the dynamics of hybrid selling, the whole 'system' cannot work properly. Let's look at what the scores mean and how they interrelate.

Essentials

If you scored low, you are essentially trying to build without foundations. Salespeople must understand how to plan and prepare, structure a call, write a proposal and follow up. They must also be clear on who they are going to interact with and why.

It is surprising how many salespeople are expected to perform (or, themselves, think they can) with no formal training. Many individuals and organisations also take a 'been there, done that' attitude to development and have nothing in place to reinforce the fundamentals. Look at top performers in the world of sport and how they practise every single day. There is something to learn there.

If you scored high, it means you are likely to have had good initial training, reinforcement through coaching and a plan to implement this learning. It is also likely you keep up your professional development with formal training or by reading books, watching videos, listening to podcasts and generally using the huge quantity of information that is out there. Sales and an understanding of the basics is continually developing with advances in neuroscience and ways to research what works best in an ever-changing environment. New technology also means that what was traditionally considered best practice is also shifting. You are aware of this and want to keep up to date.

Virtual selling

If you scored low, you may be uncomfortable with the technology that can now be employed to assist in selling. Indeed, you might find it a little frightening. You may be stuck in the past and insistent that sales can only be done face to face and in person. Citing 'it's what the customer wants' is often an excuse, as this is usually not true – they want the most effective way to operate and get to the outcomes they require.

If you scored high, you are embracing the ways that technology can assist in what you do. You understand that things change, and we must progress. You are comfortable talking on camera, whether live or recording video that can be sent to customers as an integrated part of your sales process or used on social media. Indeed, social media is a regular part of your sales activity and you create useful content, post and comment on a consistent basis. Essentially, you know that doing these things demonstrates you have a grasp of new ways of working and how these contribute to and are key in developing your personal brand.

Opportunity management

If you scored low, you probably have an ad hoc way of winning new business. This does not necessarily mean that you are not keen and do not do the right things; it usually means your approach is unstructured. Two significant dangers of working like this are that you can miss important information, and that actions are based mainly on what and who you do know rather than what and who you should. By not applying the necessary thinking it is possible that you work on projects that are dreams rather than real opportunities, as you fail to qualify them strongly enough, initially.

A high score shows you have a good structure for understanding and working with stakeholders, both internal and external. You appreciate the value of good information and make this a focus in selling activity, whether through obtaining it or sharing it. Much of your own decision making is about how the customer makes decisions and facilitating this. Your actions are well thought-out and based on deciding what will make the biggest difference. Implementation or mutual action plans are part of your way of working as you recognise that sharing these shows capability and credibility, to keep up momentum and drive success.

Leading

A low score shows that you might be somewhat reactive to customers. Alternatively, you might be too focused on your own process or systems to do the things that customers actually care about or find valuable. You are in danger of trying to satisfy only your own needs and not contributing anything useful, of telling customers what they already know or do not need to know. Self-centred selling activity may come from a lack of understanding about how people buy, or from not appreciating that increasingly it is customer focus and helping the customer to work more effectively that really sets salespeople apart.

If you scored high in this, it indicates you have the customer's best interests at heart and are prepared to help them achieve what is best for them. You know that this can come from helping them make sense of complicated and confusing situations, including their own buying process. You have a good understanding of change and what it entails and while probably an 'initiator' yourself, you recognise that others approach change differently. When appropriate you can challenge others and inspire action.

Value selling

Scoring low shows you do not use a key component of professional selling as effectively as you might. Whether deliberate or through lack of training this puts you at a disadvantage as without seeing value a customer is unlikely to buy. Maybe you do not appreciate just how important this is today or have been brainwashed during product training and directed to go and tell people 'stuff'. People do not want to know about something unless it is relevant to them and, even then, what something does will not be as interesting as what it could do *for them*. Consider whether you bring any new thinking to the table and why someone would want to talk to you, bearing in mind that information about your 'stuff' is most likely available online. Also ask whether you are spending enough time talking to customers about whether they are getting what they want from working with you.

A high score means you have a good customer focus and understand how salespeople need to work today. You recognise that value is determined by customers, and information you provide is intended to stimulate discussion to discover this. You are aware that perceptions of value change and try to keep on top of this with constant recalibration. In fact, you are comfortable introducing information that might change these perceptions and this is part of your role in adding value (as opposed to feeling that you risk undoing all your previous work by telling the customer too much). In understanding value, you make discussing price, or investment, easier.

Expanding

A low score indicates a 'won and done' approach. This might be a result of an organisation's structure, where account management and customer success are handed over to others. Or it might reflect your attitude to selling. If this is the case and responsibility for looking after customers resides with you, then you miss the point about growing business (with both current and referred customers). Your lack of customer focus could be down to a lack of self-discipline and not knowing how to get the most out of your time.

If you scored high, it shows that you understand and value customer relationships as a means of generating business. These relationships are based on maintaining contact generally and in specifically checking whether customer expectations are being met. You are able to manage yourself and make decisions based on deadlines and impact. As well as wanting to grow business it is highly likely that you also want to grow yourself and take a keen interest in self-development and anything that will help you sell better.

Questions to ask yourself

The basic question is 'So what you gonna do about it?'

You have taken the time and effort to assess your skills and approach and begun to understand what the core elements of hybrid selling are. To get the benefit from this it is important to reflect on how you can use this understanding to develop a better version of yourself.

These questions are designed to help you reflect and begin to draw up a plan to develop your hybrid selling skills:

- What insights has this self-assessment provided regarding the way you sell?

- Are the areas where you scored 'low' problem areas for you? If so, how can you address them (eg training, practice, invest in better systems or materials)?

- How have your weaknesses hurt you in your current way of selling?

- Based on your self-assessment, prioritise your three weakest elements – the first listed being the one you want to improve the most.

- How can you build on an area you are strong in?

- Who do you know that is good at an area of hybrid selling in which you are weak? What can you learn from them?

- What might hold you back from keeping up to date with how you work?

- How can you ensure you are always developing your hybrid selling skills?

Summary

You should now understand more about yourself and how you can develop to make the most of using a hybrid selling approach.

You can decide where to focus your energy to become a more rounded and complete sales professional who can be successful in today's selling environment.

The key elements of the EVOLVE framework will help with this:

- Having a strong basis in the Essentials of selling

- Using technology to factor Virtual, video and social selling into your daily activity

- Managing Opportunities through using structure and information

- Leading and guiding customers in activities relevant to them

- Focusing on understanding, positioning and communicating Value

- Expanding the business by applying account management plus customer success and personal growth principles

14
Making A Difference

I have said it before, and I will say it again; sales is
about action.

This section is designed to act as a quick reference for
the things that you can do to really get your hybrid
selling activity up to speed. It is purposefully presented like a checklist.

Look at the points and consider whether you can do
any of them better. Make a note, highlight, keep a log,
tell someone – whatever is going to make you commit
to do something about improving.

The Brindis mantra is 'think/learn/do' with a heavy
accent on DO as selling and sales development is

about results. Consider how you can make the key elements of this book work for you.

Make a commitment to act.

Think/learn/do

Thinking

The good news is loads of thinking about best practice in selling has been done for you already. There has been plenty of research undertaken, reports published, models developed and books written on the subject. Indeed, I have distilled much of this into the EVOLVE model for hybrid selling so that you can concentrate on deciding what you are going to do, when and how. The main things for you to think about are:

Essentials

- Understanding the past trends in selling and what is useful today

- Using the VALUE framework as a means of codifying and developing their approach:

  - Validate – how to check an opportunity is the right fit for doing business

  - Align – how we can work together

- Leverage – how to make a sales approach

- Underpin – how to present, prove and agree

- Evolve – how to develop the business

- Developing partnering skills to drive ethos and behaviours in today's sales environment

Virtual selling

- Becoming excellent at running online meetings using video conference technology

- Recording, sending and posting videos

- Making the most of the opportunity social media offers to improve communication and customer contact

- Using tools to help with some of the tasks machines can do better and faster

- Taking the opportunity to learn and develop with the assistance available

Opportunity management

- Qualifying projects or chances to win business

- Assessing competition (including status quo)

- Positioning the offer from a customer perspective

- Understanding who is involved in the decision and how to deliver what they need/want

- Deciding on the best actions to take

- Using mutual action plans to demonstrate competence and drive activity to enable outcomes

Leading

- Acting as a servant leader

- Focusing on and assisting with buying journeys

- Generating and sharing insight

- Using VUCA Prime to structure thinking and develop a joint approach

Value selling

- Defining what value means for the customer

- Positioning what you can do in a way that is meaningful in relation to the customer's definition

- Generating insight to drive discussion that explores ways a customer can benefit

- Pricing and negotiating based on outcomes for the customer

Expand

- Using good account management practices

- Building relationships with customers

- Focusing on customer success and delivering results

- Employing self-management techniques to focus on high-impact activity

- Keeping well – physically and mentally

- Reflecting on how to develop personally

Learning

More good news! There are also loads of ways for you to learn the necessary skills for today's selling. I don't think there has ever been a time when so much is available in so many formats. And so much of it is free.

Of course, it requires an investment of time and the discipline to apply and adopt new ways of working. You are reading this, so it is highly likely that you are receptive to new ideas and have probably consumed information from a number of sources including:

- Books

- Videos

- Podcasts

- Blogs

- Documentaries

- Apps

- Webinars

- Panel discussions

- Training courses

- Conferences

Don't forget that other valuable sources to learn from are:

- Friends and family

- Colleagues

- Customers

- Coaches

- Communities

- Accountability groups

What are you using now? Are you really getting the most out of them by taking the ideas and using them?

Doing

The secret is in implementation rather than information.

I see people boast they have read a book a week for a year. Admirable, but potentially pointless if the ideas and the learning are not applied. If you are able to take an action point and make it work for you this is when you will reap the rewards. However, this is not always easy. I have just said how much information is now available: there is often a 'shiny new thing' that comes along. It can be a distraction and, in a world where attention spans are shortening, the promise of a 'hack' or quick fix can be extremely alluring.

The discipline required for good selling is quite similar to that needed for good learning. Take time to identify what is valuable and how it can make a difference, commit to doing it, work hard to make it happen and drive the results. A plan of action and implementation helps. We are essentially talking about outcome enablement for ourselves.

Using the fundamental sales skill of questioning provides a basic structure for this:

- **What** (the thing to focus on)
- **Why** (the benefit of doing it)
- **When** (the deadline to achieve it)
- **How** (the steps and things to do to make it happen)
- **Who** (the assistance required)

This is simple but it works better than just having an idea, then another, then another, then another.

Making it happen

So what are you going to do about it?

To get the most out of this book you need to:

- Capture 'aha moments' – noting things that will make a difference and committing to do something, which includes the smaller things that add up to make a bigger difference (it is easier to do 100 things 1% better than 1 thing 100% better)

- Reflect on current knowledge – thinking about whether you already know something and whether you actually do it

- Apply ideas in real life – committing to action as this is where learning really takes place and where results are achieved

- Push your comfort zone – trying new things and operating in your stretch zone

It is all about maximising the return on your investment. You have invested your most valuable resource, time, in reading this. What you can take away will depend on your role. People in different positions have different ways to benefit.

For the sales leader

- Introduce the team to hybrid selling:
  - How can you ensure they have the right ethos to work this way?
  - What skills are they strong in already?
  - How can skills be developed?
- Review current sales practices and consider new, more effective approaches:
  - Are there any serious gaps?
  - Where can small adjustments deliver big gains?
- Look at internal alignment with other departments to ensure they support this type of sales approach:
  - Who works most closely with the sales team?
  - How effectively can different parties collaborate?
- Consider your leadership style:
  - Are you using a variety of skills in your management approach?
  - For which of the elements of hybrid selling can you act as a role model?

For the salesperson

- Sense-check your sales ethos to see if it is in line with hybrid selling skills:
  - Is your thinking consistent with a hybrid sales approach?
  - How does this reflect in your behaviours?
- Apply your 'aha moments':
  - How can you use the '1% improvements' you have identified?
  - What will be the impact of aggregating marginal gains?
- Adopt a whole new approach; take the plunge to introduce some radical transformations to get up to date:
  - What would be the gains from doing so?
  - What does the 'new you' look like?
  - What are the steps you must take to achieve this?
  - How can you take these?
  - When will you take them?
  - Whose help might you need?

Whatever role you play, identify areas for quick wins using the Summary section of each chapter.

Highlight areas you want to adopt in the coming weeks and months and be clear on 'why, what and how' to make it happen.

Don't go it alone

Implementing changes can be daunting; we have explored this already. But where there is a will there is a way.

Your relationships are highly relevant to your personal development. It is useful to think about how you can:

1. **Involve your colleagues** – Choose the ones who you can already recognise to be using elements of a hybrid selling approach and work with them. Give them the self-assessment, share ideas and create plans to develop your skills together and use them with customers.

2. **Involve your customers** – either 'covertly' by trying new approaches which use greater levels of hybrid selling or 'overtly' by telling them how you are trying to conduct business. As this is about mutual benefit either way would be acceptable.

3. **Involve me** – I would love to hear how you are getting on and whether I can help in any way. I would also appreciate any feedback you have.

Please do get in touch. My contact details are in the Resources section at the end of this book.

Summary

'Gerron wi' yit,' as we say in Nottinghamshire – in other words: act. Do something.

It is all very well knowing something, planning something or even deciding something. We will not get results until we DO SOMETHING. This advice should be clear now so:

- Use the EVOLVE action checklist

- Consult the masses of resources available to keep learning

- Draw up and implement a plan to make your learning come to life

- Involve other people to help you implement ideas

15
The Future

Have I got a crystal ball? No.

Can I confidently predict that sales and the way we need to operate are changing? Yes.

Do I think that the salesperson of the future is going to be a far more sophisticated, all-round individual needing skills in a variety of areas? Yes. It is why I have written this book, after all.

Perhaps this goes against a trend in some parts of selling: to 'optimise' the sales process and allocate different parts to separate roles held by various individuals. We will see.

While it is important to do things with the customer in mind, I am happy to see salespeople be a little self-centred in one area – their own development – and indeed encourage them to do this.

This section is written with that in mind. To encourage reflection on what, or indeed who you want to be; and to inspire action. By now I'm sure you would expect nothing else!

Who will you be?

Choose your future

More importantly, who do you want to be?

Ultimately, it is your choice and down to you how you make that happen.

We are at a unique point in history. The speed of change is perhaps faster than ever before and the rule book (if there ever was one) has been thrown away. The opportunity for personal growth and professional success is massive.

Fill the vacuum

Early in my career, I was given advice to 'fill the vacuum'. Initially I thought this a version of 'It's easier to seek forgiveness than ask permission'. But it is not. It is about taking the opportunity to do the things that other people are not doing. It is about maximising your own potential by taking ownership of the things that will make a difference; making yourself valuable.

Long gone are the days of a steady, predictable career. The times when you might stay with a company forever, expect to be routinely promoted on a regular basis and be presented with a watch halfway through and a carriage clock at the end.

It's funny how timepieces were chosen as the symbols of achievement and how people spoke of experience as 'time served'. That is not so relevant now. Results are far more important.

This should be an easy enough concept for a salesperson to grasp as essentially it is what we sell – or should be, anyway. We can take the idea and apply it to ourselves and our personal development, use it as a means to focus on preparing to be the person that can deliver results. Think of your career and progression as outcomes and undertake the activities to achieve this.

Competitive advantage

Rather than waiting for development opportunities to be handed to you on a plate and then fighting against them (I have seen too many salespeople approach training as if it were an inconvenience) a top sales professional will seek them out. They want to learn, they want to stay ahead of the game, they want to be different.

The time to make yourself different is now and hybrid selling is the opportunity to do this. By focusing on and developing the skills today's salesperson requires to be successful you develop your own competitive advantage.

There is lots of talk about 'personal branding' at the moment and I believe it goes deeper than posting decent content on particular platforms. A brand should be built on substance. You must be able to walk the talk.

Personal branding

A simple framework for considering your personal brand comprises three elements – purpose, practice, profile.

Purpose is about why we do what we do. Those who can align their work with their values and beliefs will naturally be more driven. Their job becomes more than a wage. They are happier and the impetus that drives them is reflected in what they say and do.

Practice can also be considered as 'performance'. Things get done and done well. Reputation is built on action.

Profile is good communication and involves the use of social media as a means to get the message out. Some people with great purpose and practice don't let enough other people know – this is a shame. Some people without the substance to back things up make a lot of noise – this is also a shame.

It is a question of balance.

Summary

Where are you going?

Now is the time to consider your destiny. The rules have changed, and you can take the opportunity to plan your journey.

Recognising that hybrid selling is both a model you can use for success and a means to manage your personal development is a first step.

Taking ownership can help you develop your competitive advantage and personal brand. By doing the things others are not you can set yourself apart in ways that have meaning for your company, your customers and above all to yourself.

Carpe diem.

Conclusion

What a time to be in sales!

At the outset, I said I thought that it is an exciting time to be involved in this profession as there are huge opportunities out there. However, there is a caveat to this, which is expressed in the old expression 'Fortune favours the brave'. Today it is those who are brave enough to accept that things have changed and that they too must change who will make the most of the potential out there.

Easy for me to say? Maybe. But it is also something that I have done.

I have fundamentally changed the way I work, to equip and develop salespeople to be more effective.

Gone are the days of the long classroom sessions spread over three, four or even five days. No more mammoth meetings in conference centres and hotels. An end to hours spent filling training participants with vast amounts of knowledge in one go (though there may be occasion for some conference-type events and 'boot camp'-style preparation, but these will be massively reduced).

Instead, the changes we have experienced mean that shorter, punchier sessions are now the order of the day. Virtual instructor-led training (VILT) delivered livestreamed from a studio with elements added to encourage application and adoption are the preferred option.

My Collaborative Selling Accelerator already incorporates a number of elements with this in mind, including:

- Live VILT training sessions
- Live coaching and blockbuster sessions
- Sales/buying enablement platform
- Video and digital support
- Online community
- AI-driven coaching chatbot
- Partnering skills self-audit

- Collaborative selling scorecard

- Podcasts

- Book

The Accelerator works by driving activity informed by an understanding of the VALUE framework. The content is up to date and so is the means of delivery. Pure knowledge is not enough any more. Customers require results and need to know the outcomes. Implementation beats information.

I am talking about what I sell, and I am also talking about what you sell. If we are serious about selling and want to maintain a professional approach we need to keep adapting. Change is happening perhaps faster than ever before, so we need to keep up to date. An already demanding role is becoming increasingly demanding. But it doesn't have to be difficult.

A smart salesperson will understand that they need to bring multiple skills to the table. They appreciate that it is not 'one size fits all' and they are ready to adjust their activity to what is relevant at the time. Being able to do this means they are equipped to be relevant. They have the tools and techniques at their disposal. They understand hybrid selling.

What a time to be in sales!

Epilogue

Back to winning ways

So, what of our friends from Part 1? How are they getting on?

Well, a recent conversation they had went like this:

HARRY: Hi, Larry.

LARRY: How are you doing, Harry?

HARRY: Whoa! You're looking good!

LARRY: Cheers. I've upgraded my kit. New camera, lighting, mic.

HARRY: Nice. You've upgraded your smile, too.

LARRY: I'm in a much happier place.

HARRY: So you should be, you are doing a good job.

LARRY: How do you know that?

HARRY: I was talking to one of your customers. Anyway, what else have you been doing to make your selling better?

LARRY: Well, one of the things I did was go back and look at all of the essentials for success that we spoke about a little while ago. And I realised that I am good at those things. So I doubled down on the things I know still make a difference, and then looked to see how I could develop new ways of working to get things more up to date.

HARRY: OK, so what did you do?

LARRY: Well, I looked at virtual selling. And as you can see I've really taken that to heart. I'm quite comfortable doing meetings online now. In fact, I like it. It's making me way more productive. And I know that customers actually like it too, which is a pretty good thing.

HARRY: Yeah, it's true, they do.

LARRY: I've also got far better at recording video and sending that and using it in social media.

HARRY: Yeah, I know, I've seen some of your posts. They're really good.

LARRY: Well, it makes so much sense to do it. I know that when people can see and hear you, they can start to feel they know you better. So I use video when prospecting and I use it when I'm posting on social media so that I can get my brand, my personality, out there. Now it makes a lot of sense.

HARRY: What else is happening?

LARRY: Well, remember you told me about the opportunity management model? I've started using it. I didn't realise how much information I was missing: all the things I thought I knew but didn't.

HARRY: So true.

LARRY: What I also didn't realise was how much extra information my colleagues have. It's a bit like a jigsaw, and they've got loads of the pieces that I don't, but when we bring it together, we can make the whole picture far clearer and do a far better job. I really like working in that way, as it brings the team together far better. I feel as though I'm actually leading the sale.

HARRY: I've always said you're a good leader, Larry.

LARRY: Yeah, the leadership piece we spoke about is important. Not just internally, but with the customers as well. I was surprised at how many of them don't really know how to buy. But then I suppose, if they're not buying the things that we sell regularly, why should they know the process? And I found that the help I can give them, taking them through the steps and the considerations they need to make, is really valuable for them. It makes quite a difference, just doing that.

HARRY: I'm with you on that one. Totally makes so much sense! What else you up to?

LARRY: Oh well, I've started to reward myself with Scooby snacks.

HARRY: What are you talking about, Scooby snacks?

LARRY: Scooby Doo eats them.

HARRY: Yes, I know what Scooby snacks are.

LARRY: Well, remember we were saying 'value is a mystery' and we talked about the whole Mystery Machine thing? Well, I've really started to think of selling value more like that. I've started to uncover it with customers and basically when I've done a good job I just give myself a little reward. I call these my Scooby snacks.

HARRY: *[Laughs]* Right, I've got you. Value selling makes so much more sense when you approach it like that. Anything else?

LARRY: Well, I've always thought I was good at business development, but what I found now is that I can be even more considered and even more deliberate in the way that I share information with people, that is going to make a difference for them. I'm doing a better job at keeping in touch. I've got a whole contact plan that I use, so now I know that I'm never going to forget to connect with somebody, even if we're not working on a current project together.

HARRY: It sounds as though you're doing a really good job. I'm really pleased for you.

LARRY: Once I realised that selling is changing and with those changes there is huge potential, I embraced it and now I'm seeing the difference.

HARRY: Your customers are seeing the difference too and the best thing is, I can see it in you, too.

LARRY: I've got you to thank for a lot of that.

HARRY: No problem, it's what we do. We are professional salespeople. We are here to serve.

Bibliography

Brown, W, 'Get Out of the Position of Supplier', Selling Through Partnering Skills podcast (1 October 2020)

Copestake, F, *Selling Through Partnering Skills: A modern approach to winning business* (AuthorHouse, 2020)

Dent, S, *Partnering Intelligence: Creating value for your business by building smart alliances* (Davies-Black Publishing, 1999)

Disney, Daniel, 'The Essential Guide to Social Selling', LinkedIn (22 January 2018), https://www.linkedin.com/pulse/essential-guide-social-selling-daniel-disney/, accessed 24 September 2021

Gartner, *New B2B Buying Journey & Its Implication for Sales* (Gartner 2021), available at www.gartner.com/en/sales/insights/b2b-buying-journey, accessed 25 August 2021

Greenleaf, RK, *The Power of Servant Leadership* (Berrett-Koehler, 1998)

Hatfield, C, 'Mental Wellbeing and Sales Performance', Selling Through Partnering Skills podcast (7 July 2021)

Johansen, B, *Get There Early: Sensing the future to compete in the present* (Berrett-Koehler, 2007)

Johansen, B, *Leaders Make the Future: Ten new leadership skills for an uncertain world* (Berrett-Koehler, 2007; 2nd edn 2012)

Lessard, T, 'Video in Selling: Build trust faster', Selling Through Partnering Skills podcast (5 April 2021)

Low, A and Turley, R, 'Social Selling Explained', Down the Rabbit Hole podcast (19 March 2021)

Martinez Jr, M, 'Video in Selling: Fools and tools?', Selling Through Partnering Skills podcast (5 April 2021)

Miller, RB, Heiman, SE and Tuleja, T, *The New Strategic Selling: The unique sales system proven successful by the world's best companies* (Grand Central Publishing, 2008; 3rd edn Kogan Page, 2011)

Sheridan, M and Lessard, T, *The Visual Sale: How to use video to explode sales, drive marketing, and grow your business in a virtual world* (Ideapress Publishing, 2020)

Wilkinson, M and Macdivitt, H, *The Seven Challenges of Value* (Abramis, 2017)

Williams, T, 'Mutual Action Plans Get a Makeover', Selling Through Partnering Skills podcast (31 May 2021)

Notes

1. Bob Johansen, *Leaders Make the Future: Ten new leadership skills for an uncertain world* (San Francisco: Berrett-Koehler, 2007; 2nd edn 2012)
2. Edward K Strong Jr, *The Psychology of Selling* (McGraw-Hill, 1925)
3. Dale Carnegie, *How to Win Friends and Influence People* (Simon & Schuster, 1936)
4. Quoted in Percy H Whiting, *The Five Great Rules of Selling* (McGraw-Hill, 1947)
5. Taken from Lexico, www.lexico.com/definition/underpin, accessed 25 August 2021
6. Steve Dent, Steve Dent, *Partnering Intelligence: Creating Value for your business by building smart alliances* (Davies-Black Publishing, 1999)
7. J Hale and J Grenny, 'How to get people to actually participate in virtual meetings', *Harvard*

Business Review (March 2020), available at
https://hbr.org/2020/03/how-to-get-people-
to-actually-participate-in-virtual-meetings,
accessed 21 October 2021

8. Marcus Sheridan and Tyler Lessard, *The Visual Sale: How to use video to explode sales, drive marketing, and grow your business in a virtual world* (Ideapress Publishing, 2020)

9. C Newberry and K Olafson 'Social selling: what it is, why you should care and how to do it right', Hootsuite Blog (26 May 2021), https://blog.hootsuite.com/what-is-social-selling/, accessed 11 November 2021

10. Alexander Low, Death of a Salesman podcast, https://alexanderlow.podbean.com

11. Daniel Disney, *The Ultimate LinkedIn Sales Guide* (Wiley, 2021)

12. US Department of Defense, 'DoD News Briefing - Secretary Rumsfeld and Gen. Myers', DoD (12 February 2012), available at https://archive. ph/20180320091111/http://archive.defense. gov/Transcripts/Transcript.aspx?Transcript ID=2636#selection-401.0-401.53, accessed 15 November 2021

13. Gartner, 'New B2B Buying Journey & its Implication for Sales' (Gartner 2021), www. gartner.co.uk/en/sales/insights/b2b-buying-journey, accessed 23 September 2021

14. Thomas Williams and Thomas Saine, *The Seller's Challenge* (Strategic Dynamics, 2018); *Buying-Centred Selling* (Strategic Dynamics, 2019)

15. Sir Winston Churchill, Edward Fraser and Sir John Fortescue, *Serve to Lead: The British Army's manual on leadership*, with an introduction by Robin Matthews (Indie Books, 2012)

16. Robert K Greenleaf, 'What is Servant Leadership?', Robert K. Greenleaf Center for Servant Leadership, available at www.greenleaf.org/what-is-servant-leadership, accessed 21 October 2021

17. Larry Spears, *Insights on Leadership: Service, stewardship, spirit, and servant-leadership* (Wiley, 1998)

18. Gartner, 'New B2B Buying Journey & its Implication for Sales' (Gartner 2021), www.gartner.co.uk/en/sales/insights/b2b-buying-journey, accessed 23 September 2021

19. Gartner, 'New B2B Buying Journey & Its Implication for Sales' (Gartner 2021), www.gartner.co.uk/en/ sales/insights/b2b-buying-journey, accessed 23 September 2021

20. Elisabeth Kübler-Ross, Kübler-Ross Change Curve™, Elisabeth Kübler-Ross Foundation (no date), available at www.ekrfoundation.org/5-stages-of-grief/change-curve

21. Bob Johansen, *Leaders Make the Future: Ten new leadership skills for an uncertain world* (San Francisco: Berrett-Koehler, 2007; 2nd edn 2012)

22. Mike Wilkinson and Harry Macdivitt, *The Seven Challenges of Value* (Abramis, 2017)

23. Mike Wilkinson and Harry Macdivitt, *The Seven Challenges of Value* (Abramis, 2017)
24. W Brown 'Get out of the position of supplier', Selling Through Partnering Skills podcast (1 October 2020)
25. Cisco, *Cisco Customer Success Manager Specialist v1.0.0 – Student guide 2017* (Cisco, 2017) p 17
26. UNCrushed, Research Findings: *Burnout in the sales industry* (8 October, 2019), www.uncrushed.org/content/2019/10/8/research-findings-burnout-in-the-sales-industry-uncrushed-survey, accessed 23 September 2021
27. C Hatfield 'Mental wellbeing and sales performance', Selling Through Partnering Skills podcast (7 July 2021)

Contact And Resources

Please get in touch. Ask questions, share success stories, or let me know what you think of the book.

✉ fred@brindis.co.uk

Feel free to connect, share, like and comment on posts. I will endeavour to do the same:

in www.linkedin.com/in/fredcopestake

For more information and access to resources, visit:

🌐 www.hybridselling.co.uk

You can find the latest thoughts about sales and sales leadership in general here:

🌐 www.brindis.co.uk/blog

Listen to discussion and material to support and develop modern salespeople at:

🎙 https://linktr.ee/fredcopestake

Follow me on social media:

🐦 @FredCopestake

f @FredCopestake

📷 @FredCopestake

Information on general sales performance development, including training, coaching and consulting, can be found here:

🌐 www.brindis.co.uk

Acknowledgements

I would like to take this opportunity to express massive thanks to those who have helped me with this project. I am truly fortunate to be able to interact with so many people who have an impact on how I think and what I do – so many sales professionals, consultants and individuals from other areas that provide inspiration and insight.

As I try to appreciate all those that make a difference, these special people come to mind:

For our valuable discussions and providing a foreword – David Brock

For helping with your comments on content, copy and format – Clare O'Shea, James Muir, Malvina

El-Sayegh, Moeed Amin, Tom Williams and Trent Peek

For the illustrations and helping bring Harry and Larry to life – John Montgomery and Dave MacDonald

For keeping me on track through the writing and publication process – Lucy McCarraher, Joe Gregory and the team at Rethink Press

For inspiring me with your thinking you so kindly share – all the guests on the Selling Through Partnering Skills podcast

For allowing me to offer my thinking to a wider audience and sharing my aims of helping salespeople get better – all the podcast hosts who have invited me as a guest

For keeping me accountable and 'directionally correct' – Austin Nicholas, David C Hall, Jan Mikulin and Roseanna Croft (plus Daniel Priestley for providing this direction)

For supporting me in this and all parts of my work (and life!) – Donna Copestake

Finally, for allowing me over the years to fine tune my thoughts on how to best help salespeople, your engagement, enthusiasm and success makes it a pleasure to work with you – clients all over the world.

ACKNOWLEDGEMENTS

Gracias   *Obrigado*   *Shukran*

Hvala   *Tak*   *Merci*   *Danke*

Efharisto   *Mahalo*   *Grazie*

Arigato   *Spasiba*   *Kop Khun*

The Author

Fred Copestake is the founder of Brindis, a sales training consultancy.

Over the last twenty-two years, he has worked in thirty-six countries and with more than ten thousand salespeople, delivering projects that range from developing sales skills for Middle Eastern healthcare companies, to account development and sales leadership in Latin America and Europe for IT and engineering multinationals.

In 2020, he authored the book *Selling Through Partnering Skills: A modern approach to winning business.* This forms the basis for his work with sales professionals involved in complex B2B sales to ensure what they do works today and has maximum impact.

Always focusing on the desired outcomes, Fred's approach sees him work with his clients to discover new and more powerful ways to do business, build mutually beneficial relationships with their customers and increase revenue. Put simply, his work helps people and businesses improve their sales approach so they will achieve better results.

When Fred is not delivering training to UK or international clients, he can be found enjoying rugby, cricket and time with his wife.

His unique name allows him to use @fredcopestake on LinkedIn, Facebook, Instagram and Twitter.

Lightning Source UK Ltd.
Milton Keynes UK
UKHW022049060122
396707UK00004B/51